The Authors

Maralene and Miles Wesner are multi-talented teachers and prolific writers. They have published more than 150 Audio-Visual Education aids, and pioneered new reading methods with their Phonics in a Nutshell (1965).

They have written articles, and mission studies for Southern Baptist periodicals. They were in the original group of writers to develop WMU's Big "A" Club material.

They've published several books with Broadman Press: *A Fresh Look at the Gospel* (1983); *You Are What You Choose* (1984); and *How To Be a Saint When You Feel Like a Sinner* (1986) and self-published 30 books by Diversity Press.

They are noted for their no-nonsense style, their clear illustrations, and their willingness to face controversial issues. From the dual perspectives of both academic and religious professions, they seek to be a bridge between the spiritual and the intellectual worlds.

They hold Masters Degrees (MEd) from Oklahoma University plus work toward a Doctorate. Miles also attended Southwestern Baptist Theological Seminary, and served as a high school counselor. He has been the bi-vocational pastor of a small rural church for more than 50 years.

Both Maralene and Miles taught in public school and collages and served as educational consultants. Maralene taught Psychology and Speech for Southeastern Oklahoma State University for 32 years. She was chosen Oklahoma Teacher of the Year in 1975.

They have planned, led tours, and done research in all of the 50 states, Canada, Mexico, Europe, Egypt, Japan, and the Holy Land. In 1985, they were among a small group of Americans who were invited by Dr. Joseph P. Kennedy of the US/China Education Foundation and Bishop Ting, leader of the Three Self Movement, to participate in the First Symposium on the Church in Nanjing, China.

Now, they use their lifetime of varied experiences to write insightful sermons, essays, and books.

SERMONS FOR *Special* DAYS

Maralene & Miles Wesner

© 2021
Published in the United States by Nurturing Faith, Macon, GA.
Nurturing Faith is a book imprint of Good Faith Media (goodfaithmedia.org).
Library of Congress Cataloging-in-Publication Data is available.

ISBN: 978-1-63528-127-9

All rights reserved. Printed in the United States of America.

Scripture quotations are from New Revised Standard Version Bible, copyright © 1989 National Council of the Churches of Christ in the United States of America. Used by permission. All rights reserved worldwide.

Scriptures marked KJV are taken from the KING JAMES VERSION (KJV): KING JAMES VERSION, public domain.

Cover image by David Cassady.

Contents

Introduction 1

The New Year
    New Life in a New Year 4
    How Time Flies! 9
    This Is Your Moment 13
    On Smelling Roses 17
    Leave It Behind! 20

Easter
    The Victory of Easter 26
    Losers Who Win! 30
    Where Is the Risen Christ? 33
    The Demands of Easter 37
    The Lessons of Easter 41

Mother's Day
    Pointers for Parents 46
    The ABCs of Parenting 50
    Changing the Course of History 53
    Parenting 101 56
    How to Correct Your Kids 59

Father's Day
    I Do! I Really Do! 64
    Children Are Different 68
    How to Bless Your Family 70
    How to Challenge Your Children 74
    What Is Love to a Child? 78

Graduation
    The Gospel According to Humpty Dumpty 82
    Life Is a Game, and Here Are the Rules 86
    I Have Finished My Course! 90
    Just Say "Nope!" 94
    Winning the Game of Life 98

Independence Day
- I Don't Know, and I Don't Care! 104
- Free to Be Me 108
- How to Realize Our Responsibilities 112
- Keeping America Great 116
- The Star-Spangled Banner 120

Halloween
- Removing Your Mask 126
- The Real Me 131
- How to Get Rid of Your Ghosts 135
- Which Mask Do You Wear? 139
- Masks (A Children's Sermon) 144

Thanksgiving
- An Attitude of Gratitude 146
- We Must Be Thankful 150
- An Ungrateful Heart 154
- Thankful Thoughts 158
- Be Ye Thankful 162

Christmas
- The Best Gift 168
- What Is Christmas All About? 171
- The Grinches Who Steal Christmas 174
- Why Is the World Dark? 178
- What If Christ Had Not Come? 181

Miscellaneous
- Grandparents' Day 184
- I Can! I Ought! I Will! (Labor Day) 188
- My Teacher, the Ant (Labor Day) 191
- The State of the Church 195
- The Christ Within (Palm Sunday) 199
- The Meaning of the Lord's Supper 203

Introduction

Special days often attract the greatest church attendance and thus offer the greatest opportunity for outreach. Unfortunately, many holiday and seasonal messages are shallow and sentimental.

These sermons were developed with three goals in mind: appropriateness, depth, and psychological soundness. We hope this collection of our most meaningful and successful "celebration services" will be useful to others. They are highly adaptable and require a minimum amount of preparation.

The New Year

New Life in a New Year

Welcome to the beginning of a new year.

Jesus spoke of new things. He said, "No one tears a piece from a new garment and sews it on an old garment; otherwise the new will be torn, and the piece from the new will not match the old. And no one puts new wine into old wineskins; otherwise the new wine will burst the skins and will be spilled, and the skins will be destroyed. But new wine must be put into fresh wineskins" (Luke 5:36–38).

When Jesus talks about the new and the old, he isn't concerned with clothes or beverages. Instead, he is concerned with attitudes and insights. The Pharisees were tied to the "way we've always done it." They wanted Jesus to fit into their mold. Jesus said that is as ridiculous as sewing a new patch onto an old garment. You ruin both garments. Jesus didn't come to serve as a patch, but to create an entirely new garment. He said that his teachings are like fermenting wine that cannot be put into old, brittle wine containers. The gasses of the fermenting wine would burst the old wineskins. His teachings can't be contained within the old rigid system of Judaism.

This makes sense, but strangely enough, we don't accept change any more readily than those Jews did. Now, of course, we want new phones and new cars, but we don't always want new ideas and new beliefs.

Why are we so reluctant to change?

I. Change Threatens Our Security.

Change forces us to move out of our comfort zone. We only feel right when we're reading the same Bible with the same people in the same worship service. However, comfort can lead to complacency.

Actually, we're designed to improve until the day we die: to think new thoughts, to learn new skills, to develop new technologies. Often, though, we resist taking a step forward if it means leaving behind familiar circumstances. We struggle harder to hold on to what we have now than we do to reach what we could have in the future.

Nevertheless, change is necessary. In the late 1950s an inventor presented the digital watch to the leaders of the Swiss watch industry. Those leaders rejected it because they thought they already had the best watch in the world.

The inventor then offered the watch to a Japanese company. It was an instant success. The Swiss wouldn't change, and they're being left behind.

This is a parable of what is happening in many churches. Things that worked at one time in history do not work today. Things that were right for one generation may be wrong for this one. We don't force a man to keep wearing a coat that fit him when he was a boy! Sure, it was a useful coat for the child, but it's been outgrown. As congregations we need to realize that some things have been outgrown. Someone put it this way: "There are two unbreakable commandments among Christians. The first one is, 'Thou shalt not rock the boat.' The second is, 'Thou shalt not even think about rocking the boat.'"

Nevertheless, both Jesus and Paul advocated for change. The scriptures say, "You were taught to put away your former way of life, your old self, corrupt and deluded by its lusts, and to be renewed in the spirit of your minds, and to clothe yourselves with the new self, created according to the likeness of God in true righteousness and holiness" (Eph 4:22–24).

Letting go of the old is hard—whether it's a pattern of behavior, a belief, or a way of life. Change threatens our security.

II. Change Creates Anxiety.

It's natural to fear the unknown. In fact, new ideas are often rejected simply because they're new. According to legend a banker, when asked to finance a new invention, shouted, "Get that toy out of my office." The inventor was Alexander Graham Bell. The "toy" was the telephone.

A writer sent a manuscript to a Hollywood producer who immediately rejected it. The writer was Margaret Mitchell, and the manuscript was Gone with the Wind.

A young engineer was bored with his job, so he asked if he could design a personal computer for his company. His request was rejected, so he resigned his position and started his own company. The young engineer was Steve Jobs, and his design became the Apple computer.

When the first bathtubs appeared in America, they were greeted with both personal and legal resistance. The local newspaper denounced bathtubs as a "luxurious and democratic insanity." Doctors warned patients that bathtubs were a menace to health. Philadelphia once had a public ordinance that prohibited bathing between November 1 and March 15. In 1845, Boston made bathing unlawful except when prescribed by a physician.

We can't believe such ignorance once existed, yet we often do the same thing, especially if the change involves religion. Most of the important inventions and discoveries that have changed the way people live have come into general use in the last hundred years. The world today is very different from the world of our forefathers. Many of the things now known about the way nature works and the way human beings react were not known until recently. This generation has experienced greater changes than any other.

Repeating the time-honored religious precepts without practicing the principles Jesus taught makes churches lose their credibility. People turn away from doctrines that don't make a difference in their lives.

Yet the world is desperate for spiritual renewal. Economic, social, political, mental, and emotional issues threaten the collapse of civilization. We must change! We must emphasize solutions to today's problems! The gospel supports this concept. Paul said, "But now we are discharged from the law, dead to that which held us captive, so that we are slaves not under the old written code but in the new life of the Spirit" (Rom 7:6).

We must apply the scriptures to real-life situations even though such change creates anxiety.

III. Change Brings Growth.

Several years ago, a cannery in LeSueur, Minnesota, hired an analysis to help them increase sales. The analyst said the company's vegetables were as good or better than anything else on the market. They should not be changed. However, he advised them to change the look of their cans. Soon their products were number one in the nation.

Now, the contents didn't change, but the way they were presented did. It's the same with the gospel. Some things never change. In the midst of turmoil, there remains one constant: God's nature "is the same yesterday and today and forever." (See Heb 13:8.)

The message of grace, love, and forgiveness will never change. But the way this message is presented must. We can't keep patching old garments. We must overcome our fear of insecurity and anxiety.

Basic morality doesn't change. Lying, stealing, and murdering were wrong in Genesis, and they are still wrong today. Truth, generosity, and kindness were right in Genesis, and they are still right today. But the way we teach and serve must change in order to reach people in the twenty-first century.

Are we willing to rethink our beliefs, update our vocabulary, adapt our procedures, and change with the times? If not, our witness and ministry will become unproductive. Paul was adaptable. He said, "To the Jews I became as a Jew, in order to win Jews. To those under the law I became as one under the law (though I myself am not under the law) so that I might win those under the law. To those outside the law I became as one outside the law (though I am not free from God's law but am under Christ's law) so that I might win those outside the law. To the weak I became weak, so that I might win the weak. I have become all things to all people, that I might by all means save some" (1 Cor 9:20–22).

Hanging on to yesterday is counterproductive. A couple once planned a honeymoon in Hawaii. They anticipated a lazy surf, a sun-drenched beach, and a romantic Honolulu moon.

Unfortunately, there was a mix-up. Somehow they missed their flight and ended up in the Swiss Alps. Instead of sunshine and warm ocean breezes, there were subzero temperatures and icicles hanging from the roof.

The honeymooners had to make a decision. They could remain adamant, saying, "We prepared for Hawaii, and we won't let circumstances interfere." They could wear their swimsuits and sit in the snow, or they could adapt to the new environment, buy some winter clothes, rent ski gear, throw a few logs on the fireplace, and have an interesting experience.

Likewise, we must make a decision. What we do with this new year is up to us. We can hang on to the old, or we can adapt to the new. We can close our minds and hide our heads in the sand, or we can approach each changing situation by saying, "I wonder what this person or event can teach me? I wonder if considering this point of view could make a difference in my life?"

We are not sure what changes the next year or the next century will bring, but we know there will be changes. The old must make room for the new. Paul said, "So if anyone is in Christ, there is a new creation: everything old has passed away; see, everything has become new!" (2 Cor 5:17).

Many people continue to live in misery because they're afraid of change. No matter what has happened in your past, new life is possible. Paul said, "Therefore we have been buried with him by baptism into death, so that, just as Christ was raised from the dead by the glory of the Father, we too might walk in newness of life" (Rom 6:4).

Will we stay in the darkness of sin, or will we step out into the reality of grace? That's our challenge. Let's not patch up old garments or deal with cracked wine skins. Instead, let's live a new life in a new year!

How Time Flies!

Halloween is past. Thanksgiving is past. Christmas is past. The New Year is before us. The end of the year is a time to look back, to evaluate, to reassess, and to sum up our life. As we get older, one thing is obvious—time flies! The holidays come faster, and the weeks seem shorter. A man mathematically calculated a twenty-four-hour lifetime that's a little longer than the "three score and ten" years mentioned in the Bible. He said that if one lives to be eighty years of age, here is how it would break down: If you are twenty years old, it's about 6:00 in the morning. If you are forty, then it's noon. If you are sixty years old, it is 6:00 p.m. If you're seventy, it's 9:00 p.m. If you're eighty, it's midnight.

Anyone who considers this chart has to take life more seriously. When we survey the past, we become acutely aware that time only moves in one direction. Concerning the record of the past, we are compelled to say with Pilate, "What I have written I have written" (John 19:22).

The dawn of every new year silently reminds us that the past is gone forever and cannot be recalled. During the French Revolution, Louis XVI, Marie Antoinette, and the little Dauphin were inside the palace listening to the angry mob as they hurled stones and smashed windows. Finally, the mob went away, only to return the next day. When he woke up that morning, the child asked, "Mother, is it still yesterday?" "No," she replied. "Yesterday is gone forever." What a sobering reflection!

There are many times when we would like for it to still be yesterday. One lady said to her pastor, "I never attend New Year's watch services. They make me feel a year older." However, time marches on whether we attend the services or not.

Efforts to recall and relive the past often lead people into frustration and confusion. Torn between the past and the future, they are unable to adjust to the present. Those who are wise know that once we have crossed that line, there is no turning back.

Benjamin Franklin said, "Lovest thou life? Then do not squander time, for it is the stuff out of which life is made."

Paul said, "[Make] the most of the time, because the days are evil" (Eph 5:16).

"Conduct yourselves wisely toward outsiders, making the most of the time" (Col 4:5).

How can we do that? How can we redeem the time? And how can we make the most of every opportunity?

I. We Must Set Priorities.

We must decide what's most important and what's least important for us. Scripture has much to say about choices. Moses said, "I call heaven and earth to witness against you today that I have set before you life and death, blessings and curses. Choose life so that you and your descendants may live" (Deut 30:19b).

Joshua said, "As for me and my household, we will serve the LORD" (Josh 24:15b).

Paul said, "Strive for the greater gifts" (1 Cor 12:31).

Once, a solitary figure walked the beach in a fixed pattern. He would pace one way and then another. His eyes were fixed on a metal loop at the end of a wand. The wand was wired to a set of earphones, clamped to the man's head. Occasionally, he would stop, dig in the sand, and then move on. He was a modern-day beachcomber. The apparatus indicated the presence of buried coins or metal jewelry.

An observer said, "I pitied the man because in looking for treasures that might be buried in the sand, he was missing the greater treasures which were all around him—the waves and birds and beautiful shells." Let's not overlook the best treasures in life.

In order to determine priorities, it's necessary to evaluate needs and attitudes and activities. As we look back, we can ask ourselves: Am I spending enough time on significant issues? Am I spending too much time on trivial issues? Am I wasting my time? What do I enjoy doing most? What do I appreciate having most? What do I value accomplishing most? What do I wish I had done? Given a limited time to live, what do I really want to have or experience or accomplish?

Out of these questions we can determine our future goals and activities and set our priorities.

II. We Must Say No to Unimportant Activities.

In a limited lifetime, we can't do everything. We can't even do every good thing. Therefore, we must decide among all the possible uses of our time. People are often reluctant to make these choices and commitments because in order to commit ourselves to one goal, we must let many things go. In order to open and enter one door, we must close and pass by many other doors. Jesus said, "No one can serve two masters; for a slave will either hate the one and love the other, or be devoted to the one and despise the other. You cannot serve God and wealth" (Matt 6:24).

Here are five guidelines for deciding when to say no:
1. You should say no if you feel uncomfortable with the task because of lack of ability or interest.
2. You should say no if the task will greatly interfere with your family life.
3. You should say no if the task will hinder or hurt your spiritual life in any way.
4. You should say no if you are doing it out of guilt, pride, or greed.
5. You should say no if, after prayer and meditation, you do not feel it is right for you.

Remember, you should feel called to service, not sentenced to it.

The ancient Romans thought New Year's Eve was an appropriate time to rid themselves of the old and take on the new, not just symbolically but literally. They would throw out of the windows all old or worn-out things such as frayed garments, cracked dishes, or dilapidated furniture.

This idea has merit for every day, not only for New Year's Eve. But throwing away useless and nonproductive things must go far beyond material objects. It should include the disposal of fearful and depressing thoughts, hostile and resentful feelings, and destructive and harmful habits. This will enable us to say no to unimportant activities.

III. We Must Say Yes to Important Activities.

Once there was a beggar who had no money. A kind man said, "I'll give you all I have. Here's $168." Then he said, "Wait just a minute—I do need enough for emergencies. Would you please return a little bit for my use? Perhaps $5?"

The beggar replied, "No way! I have it all now, and I'll keep it all!"

You might be thinking, "That's incredible! That's unbelievable! How ungrateful can you be?" But wait just a moment! Once, there was an individual who had no time. A loving God said, "I'll give you all I have. Here's 168 hours per week. All I ask is that you return a small portion for my use."

The individual replied, "No way! I have it all, and I'll keep it all!"

That's incredible! That's unbelievable! How ungrateful can you be? Yet this happens day after day, week after week, month after month, year after year! All over the world, people take the gift of life and time and energy and refuse to return even a small portion in worship and ministry.

What kind of world, what kind of nation, what kind of community, what kind of church could we have if every person simply returned five hours out of the 168 hours they have per week to God? Charities and churches would have volunteers; worship services would be packed; outreach and prayers would flourish.

What a dream come true for leaders and faithful members! It could be realized if all of us honestly evaluate our priorities. God gives us 168 hours per week. If we spend approximately forty hours for sleep, forty hours for work, ten hours eating, ten hours dressing, twenty hours on recreation, that leaves forty-eight hours for everything else. Surely we can spare five hours for God.

Let's evaluate our life. Think of last year: What would you do differently? What would you do less of? What would you do more of? Remember—time flies. David said, "Remember how short my time is" (Ps 89:47).

Job said, "My days are swifter than a weaver's shuttle" (Job 7:6).

James said, "Yet you do not even know what tomorrow will bring. ...For you are a mist that appears for a little while and then vanishes." (Jas 4:14).

Time flies, so let's make the most of it.

This Is Your Moment

Deuteronomy 30:15-21; Joshua 24:15

Once, Joshua delivered a brief message to his people. He said, "You have not passed this way before" (Josh 3:4).

Moses had a similar message. He said, "'You must never return that way again'" (Deut 17:16).

These messages are still valid for us today. Life moves in one direction. Time doesn't stop or reverse itself. We have never been at this place in our growth before, and we'll never be at this place again.

An anonymous poet wrote:
> I expect to pass through this world but once.
> Any good thing, therefore, that I can do,
> Or any that I can show
> To any fellow human being, let me do it now,
> Let me not defer nor neglect it,
> For I shall not pass this way again.

Paul said, "See, now is the acceptable time; see, now is the day of salvation!" (2 Cor 6:2). This is our moment, and we must use it or it will be forever gone. There's a time to do what needs to be done. If we miss this opportunity, it may be forever too late.

A modern adage says, "This is the first day of the rest of your life." As Christians we are manifesting God in this world. We are bringing in the kingdom. Since we have free will, God must wait on us before his purposes can be accomplished. Jesus said, "My time has not yet come, but your time is always here" (John 7:6).

If this is our time, what are we to do with it? If this is our moment, how should we respond to it?

I. This Is Our Time to Get Real.

When the emperor Francis Joseph of Austria was being buried, at the entrance to the crypt, the procession was halted by a voice within: "Who goes there?" Someone replied, "His most serene majesty, the Emperor Francis Joseph." The challenger said, "I know him not. Who goes there?" A second reply was made: "The ruler of Austria, the King of Hungary." Again, the challenger answered, "I know him not. Who goes there?" This time the voice without replied, "A sinful man, our brother Joseph." Then the portal was opened, and the king was laid to rest.

Daniel Webster said, "We may live like a king, but we'll die like a man!" We're all sinners! Denying that and claiming special titles won't gain us entrance into the kingdom.

So to get real we must be honest. John said, "If we say that we have no sin, we deceive ourselves, and the truth is not in us. If we confess our sins, he who is faithful and just will forgive us our sins and cleanse us from all unrighteousness" (1 John 1:8–9).

The Associated Press carried a story about a traveler who swallowed several gold nuggets in an effort to sneak past customs at an airport in India. His smuggling ploy failed when a metal detector began beeping and he was arrested. It's the same with us. We can't deceive ourselves or God.

Next, to get real we must be forgiving. Paul said, "Be kind to one another, tenderhearted, forgiving one another, as God in Christ has forgiven you" (Eph 4:32).

A wise man once said, "To increase your happiness and prolong your life, learn to forget your relatives' flaws and your friends' faults. Erase the gossip you've heard. Blot out your negative thoughts. They will only grow larger when you think about them constantly. Obliterate the evils of yesterday and write only good things upon the clean sheet which is today."

Then, to get real we must be understanding. Paul said, "We have not ceased praying for you and asking that you may be filled with the knowledge of God's will in all spiritual wisdom and understanding" (Col 1:9).

We can know God's presence. Such insight often occurs precisely when we are not seeking it! Winston Churchill called it "a zigzag streak of lightning in the brain." It's a moment of knowing. It's when what has been unknowable because of ignorance and deceit suddenly emerges clear, recognized, and known.

Yes, we can get real if we develop honesty, forgiveness, and understanding.

II. This Is Our Time to Get Busy.

If someone drove down the street throwing twenty-dollar bills out the window, you would think he was a fool. Yet, every day, most of us throw away something far, far more valuable. We toss out hour after hour of precious time. Solomon said, "Those who follow worthless pursuits have no sense" (Prov 12:11).

People waste time without ever being aware that they are actually cheating themselves. Most of us inherit over half a million hours of life. A Christian businessman once made an unforgettable statement: "You take my money and you have something I can eventually replace. But rob me of my time, and it is lost forever."

Don't waste your life! To get busy means to grow. Peter said, "Grow in the grace and knowledge of our Lord and Savior Jesus Christ" (2 Pet 3:18).

A little boy was learning to ice-skate. His frequent mishaps caused an observer to advise, "Sonny, I wouldn't stay on the ice and keep falling down. I'd just sit over here and watch for a while."

With tears rolling over his cheeks, the child looked down at the shining steel on his feet and answered indignantly, "No, ma'am. I didn't get these new skates to give up with. I got them to learn how with."

That's a valuable philosophy of life. Hard tasks are never sent for us to "give up with"; they are always intended to help us grow.

Next, to get busy, we must serve: "Whatever your hand finds to do, do it with your might" (Eccl 9:10).

Tony Meléndez was unknown until Pope John Paul II visited California in 1987. Now, those who heard him perform will never forget the young man who played the guitar and sang. What made this event so memorable is that Tony was born with no hands. He learned to play the guitar with his toes. We're to serve with what we have—our voice, our hands, our feet, our mind.

Peter said, "I have no silver or gold, but what I have I give you" (Acts 3:6).

That's all anyone can do.

Then, to get busy we must share. Jesus said, "You will be my witnesses in Jerusalem, in all Judea and Samaria, and to the ends of the earth" (Acts 1:8).

Some of us are afraid to share our faith because we're afraid someone will ask us a question we can't answer. But we don't have to know everything in order to witness. We only have to know what we have experienced.

If we're holding a loaf of bread and a starving man cries out, we wouldn't hesitate because we're afraid he might ask us some question about the nature of wheat. Instead, we'd respond with food.

Yes, we can get busy if we'll grow and serve and share.

III. This Is Our Time to Get Ready.

Once in a lifetime, each of us has an opportunity to glimpse eternity. Once in a lifetime, each of us reaches a point when life-or-death choices are required. That is our moment—our golden moment. If we refuse it, we may never have another chance. So a time to get ready is a time to stop and reflect.

Swedish chemist Alfred Nobel made a fortune by inventing a powerful explosive. When his brother died a newspaper mistakenly printed the chemist's obituary instead of his brother's. Identified in it as the man whose dynamite could cause mass destruction, he realized he might only be remembered as a merchant of death. He decided to use his fortune to establish awards for accomplishments that would benefit humanity and is now remembered for the peace prizes he gives. If we seriously reflect on our lives, we may reassess our goals and rearrange our priorities.

Next, a time to get ready is a time to choose. Moses said, "I have set before you life and death, blessings and curses. Choose life so that you and your descendants may live" (Deut 30:19).

Joshua said, "Choose this day whom you will serve" (Josh 24:15). No one can have it all. No one can serve both good and evil sides. We must choose God and give up everything that's contrary to that choice.

Then, to get ready is a time to act. Once, a man stood in front of a door to heaven for a long, long time. He was waiting for someone to go in or come out. Finally, an angel asked, "Why are you standing there?"

"Well," the hesitant man replied, "I'm waiting for the door to open."

"Oh, you don't understand," the angel explained. "This is your door, and unless you knock on that door, it will never open!" We must take the first step.

Yes, we can get ready if we'll reflect, choose, and act. Solomon realized the importance of using opportunity. He said, "For everything there is a season, and a time for every matter under heaven" (Eccl 3:1).

You see, this day, this hour, this minute will never return. It's unique and irreplaceable. We must not lose it or waste it. This is your time to feel, to change, to love, to care, to move, to live. In fact, in the book of Revelation, John foresees a point in the future when time will run out. He said, "There should be time no longer" (Rev 10:6, KJV).

We have not passed this way before, and we shall never pass this way again. These words express the whole truth of life—"never before, never again!"

This is your time. This is your moment! What will you do with it?

On Smelling Roses
Psalm 118:24

How fast did he go? Who got there first? Who won? These are the questions of the twenty-first century. Everything in our world seems to be measured by speed and deadlines. The pilot said, "Ladies and gentlemen, I've got bad news and good news. The bad news is, we're lost. The good news is, we're making excellent time."

Is that our story? If so, it's dangerous. A few years ago, a Navy jet fighter shot itself down while on a test run. The plane was flying at supersonic speed, but the shells coming from a cannon mounted on its wing were moving at subsonic speeds, so the jet actually ran into the shells it had fired seconds before. That plane was going too fast for its own good. Are we? As our stress levels rise, we approach burnout.

Too often, we hurry up and wait! The ancient Greeks had different rules for their games. When runners competed, the winner wasn't necessarily the person who crossed the finish line first. The winner was the person who crossed the finish line first with his torch still burning. That's the crucial point.

Are we so concerned with "getting there" that we neglect our spiritual torches? If so, we've lost the race, no matter how fast we may run. Once, two cargo ships were hurrying toward a downstream market. One of the ships became so obsessed with winning that it ran out of fuel and burned its cargo of lumber. Sure enough, it "won," but the victory was hollow since it had nothing left to sell.

Are we like that? Are we living our lives so frantically that when we get there—to that job or promotion or achievement—we'll have nothing left? The writer of Ecclesiastes understood the problem. He said, "I saw that under the sun the race is not to the swift, nor the battle to the strong" (Eccl 9:11).

Jesus presented an interesting paradox. He said, "Many who are first will be last, and the last will be first" (Matt 19:30).

Paul also voiced his concern. "Do you not know that in a race the runners all compete, but only one receives the prize? Run in such a way that you may win it. So I do not run aimlessly, nor do I box as though beating the air" (1 Cor 9:24, 26).

In fact, success isn't in the winning; it's in the day-to-day running. If the scriptures say anything, they say God is in our present. He is in the now! He is for today! The divine proclamation to Moses didn't say, "I was who I was!"—the God of yesterday. He didn't say, "I will be who I will be!"—the God of tomorrow. Instead, he said, "I am who I am!"—the God of the present. The God of the now! The God of today! (See Exod 3:14.)

I. We're Told to Live Today.

Jesus said, "Give us this day our daily bread" (Matt 6:11).

Don't foolishly deny yourself the basic necessities of life. Jesus ate and drank and rested and slept. So we must take care of our physical needs today!

Solomon said, "Do not boast about tomorrow, for you do not know what a day may bring." (Prov 27:1).

James said, "Yet you do not even know what tomorrow will bring. What is your life? For you are a mist that appears for a little while and then vanishes" (Jas 4:14).

These men are saying, "Don't procrastinate. Don't put things off. Don't wait for a more convenient season. It never comes." We must take advantage of today! We must live today!

II. We're Told to Serve Today.

The psalmist said, "O that today you would listen to his voice! Do not harden your hearts" (Ps 95:7–8).

The writer of Hebrews repeated this advice twice, saying, "Therefore, as the Holy Spirit says, 'Today, if you hear his voice'" (Heb 3:7).

Again, God "sets a certain day—'today'—saying through David much later, in the words already quoted, 'Today, if you hear his voice, do not harden your hearts'" (Heb 4:7).

Wake up, observe, perceive, think, and live. Don't sleep through, or dream through, or exist through, or stumble through your life. We must listen and heed God's voice today!

Paul said, "For (God) says, 'At an acceptable time I have listened to you, and on a day of salvation I have helped you.' See, now is the acceptable time; see, now is the day of salvation!" (2 Cor 6:2).

So don't wait to be your best, and do your best, and give your best. "Someday soon" becomes never. We don't become saints in our sleep. We must live out our salvation today! We must serve today!

III. We're Told to Enjoy Today.

The psalmist said, "This is the day that the LORD has made; let us rejoice and be glad in it" (Ps 118:24).

Don't be so preoccupied with saving for a rainy day that may come that you can't appreciate the sunny days you have now.

It's important to notice that Jesus enjoyed weddings and feasts and conversation with good friends.

When it comes to smelling the roses, remember this: Most of us will miss out on the really big payoffs. Few ordinary people win Nobel Prizes, Oscars, Olympic gold medals, or multimillion-dollar lotteries. Fortunately, however, we're all eligible for life's little pleasures. A smile, a pat on the back, and a compliment are available to us. The gorgeous sunsets, the majestic mountains, and the starry skies are available to us.

In fact, God has given us years full of days to appreciate and cherish.

This adaptation of an old Amish song expresses this message to each to us:

Hold on to the sound of the music of living,

Sweet songs from the laughter of children at play.

Just smell of the grass as we run through the meadow,

and cherish the memory of what is today.

Hold on to this moment; it won't be repeated.

It slips through our fingers and will not delay.

Our yesterday's gone and tomorrow's uncertain,

So cherish the memory of what is today.

As we live through the time God has given us in this new year, don't ignore the little things in your rush toward the big things. Live life now! This is the day the Lord has made; let's rejoice and be glad in it. God wants us to smell the roses!

Leave It Behind!
Genesis 19:12, 17, 24-26

In the story of the destruction of Sodom and Gomorrah, Lot, his wife, and daughters escaped. They were warned to flee the city and not look back. Lot's wife couldn't resist and, according to this legend, was immediately turned into a pillar of salt.

One writer said, "As a child hearing this story, I could never understand why that happened to her. I saw it as punishment for curiosity. I never saw the fairness in it. However, when we look at its symbolism and psychology, it makes much more sense."

When we are freed from a difficulty, it can be disastrous to keep looking back. We become immobilized, and we can't move on in our lives. Jesus said, "Let the dead bury their own dead" (Matt 8:22). He meant, "Leave the past, and move on."

A counselor asked this question, "Would you take things from yesterday's garbage to make today's dinner?" Well, of course we wouldn't, so why do we dig up old hurts and resentments and relive them over and over again?

This story of Lot and his wife tells us to leave the past behind, which can be difficult, because every gain entails a loss. When you graduate, you must leave elementary and high school behind. When you move into a new house, you must leave the old house behind. We understand that it's hard to leave comfortable and pleasant things behind, but it should be easy to leave painful and unpleasant things behind. Unfortunately, that's not always true. You see, we get conditioned to the familiar. We get so used to our faults and failures that life doesn't feel right without them. Nevertheless, dragging along a lot of baggage takes its toll.

The writer of Hebrews said it well: "Therefore, since we are surrounded by so great a cloud of witnesses, let us also lay aside every weight and the sin that clings so closely, and let us run with perseverance the race that is set before us" (Heb 12:1).

Having to deny and hide and overcompensate saps our energy and hinders our progress. Solomon spoke to this issue when he said, "No one who conceals transgressions will prosper, but one who confesses and forsakes them will obtain mercy" (Prov 28:13).

Besides, every time something triggers one of our old hurts, we become just as helpless and miserable as we were back when the original trauma occurred. That's why the scriptures tell us to leave the past behind. Jesus said, "No one who puts a hand to the plow and looks back is fit for the kingdom of God" (Luke 9:62).

So what are the "sins" and problems that we should leave behind? Well, there are guilts, fears, hostilities, regrets, and destructive habits.

I. We Should Leave Our Guilts Behind Us.

Guilts can be either helpful or harmful. When guilt comes as a warning to make us change dangerous or unproductive behavior, it's beneficial. But guilt that's unwarranted or prolonged can be demoralizing. Because of past teachings we can have false guilt. We can feel bad about things that are not really wrong. Gandhi felt guilty about eating beef because of his Hindu religion. Former Quakers may feel guilty if they wear red or blue clothing. Paul gave the example of eating meat that had been offered to the idols. He said, "There's nothing wrong with the meat, but if we feel guilty about it, we'll suffer": "The faith that you have, have as your own conviction before God. Blessed are those who have no reason to condemn themselves because of what they approve. But those who have doubts are condemned if they eat, because they do not act from faith; for whatever does not proceed from faith is sin" (Rom 14:22–23).

Guilt that's held past its point of usefulness is also demoralizing. In fact, unresolved guilt can go on doing its damage to the personality year after year. The writer of Hebrews described how the Jews had to keep offering sacrifices annually because they never felt forgiven. He said the sacrifice could not effect a permanent cure: "Otherwise, would they not have ceased being offered, since the worshipers, cleansed once for all, would no longer have any consciousness of sin?" (Heb 10:2).

Now, that's not necessary. God's forgiveness is permanent: "'I will remember their sins and their lawless deeds no more.' Where there is forgiveness of these, there is no longer any offering for sin" (Heb 10:17–18).

Living with guilt leads to obsessive and neurotic behavior. It can even lead to self-punishment. If we feel unworthy, we can actually sabotage our successes and pleasures because we don't feel we deserve them. Someone said, "Guilt doesn't stop us from sinning. It just keeps us from enjoying it." The gospel says it's possible to leave our guilts behind. God promises forgiveness and restoration: "As far as the east is from the west, so far he removes our transgressions from us" (Ps 103:12).

So let's leave our guilts behind us and get on with our lives.

II. We Need to Leave Our Fears Behind Us.

Fears can also be both helpful and harmful. They protect us by preparing us for fight or flight in times of danger, but they can linger on and inhibit us in personal, social, and business situations.

Some fears lead to debilitating conditions, such as phobias and chronic anxiety and panic attacks. It's these false fears that become so destructive.

The gospel says it's possible for us to leave our fears behind. God promises peace and serenity. "Do not worry about anything, but in everything by prayer and supplication with thanksgiving let your requests be made known to God. And the peace of God, which surpasses all understanding, will guard your hearts and your minds in Christ Jesus" (Phil 4:6–7).

"Those of steadfast mind you keep in peace—in peace because they trust in you" (Isa 26:3).

So let's leave our fears behind us and get on with our lives.

III. We Must Leave Our Hostilities Behind Us.

Hostilities can take the form of blaming others. The hostile person can become bitter and exhibit rage or plot revenge. The hostile person can also suppress his feelings and become depressed. All of these are nonproductive. One man said, "I can't stand it any longer! I've resented that guy for twenty years, and it's driving me nuts!"

"Why don't you forgive him?" his friend replied.

"Forgive him! Are you kidding? He did a terrible thing to me! I'm not going to let him off that easily!"

His friend laughed, "Let him off that easily? Why, he's probably out playing golf and doesn't even know that you resent him. When you resent people, you let them live rent-free in your head. Forgiving him would free you."

Sometimes we think remembering a hurt or holding a grudge will protect us from future pain. We're afraid if we let down our guard, we'll become weak and vulnerable. That's not necessarily true. Once we know enough to prevent a reoccurrence, we can let go of our anger. The gospel says it's possible to leave our hostilities behind. "For if you forgive others their trespasses, your heavenly Father will also forgive you" (Matt 6:14).

God promises love and reconciliation, so let's leave our hostilities behind us and get on with our lives.

IV. We Must Leave Our Regrets Behind Us.

Regrets are almost totally useless. We can't turn back the clock and redo our past. Saying "If only I'd done this" or "If only I hadn't done that" wastes time and undermines our confidence. In fact, most of us do the best we can at the moment. Hindsight may be twenty-twenty, but we shouldn't berate ourselves for mistakes we can't do anything about. John Greenleaf Whittier expressed it this way: "For of all sad words of tongue or pen; the saddest are these: 'It might have been!'"

The gospel says it's possible to leave our regrets behind. God promises confidence and hope. Paul said, "Beloved, I do not consider that I have made it my own; but this one thing I do: forgetting what lies behind and straining forward to what lies ahead" (Phil 3:13).

So let's leave our regrets behind us and get on with our lives.

V. We Must Leave Our Destructive Habits Behind Us.

Destructive habits plague everyone at times. Some are deadly, such as drug or alcoholic addictions. Others can turn into compulsions. Scripture says this makes us slaves. Paul definitely suffered from such patterns of behavior: "For we know that the law is spiritual; but I am of the flesh, sold into slavery under sin. I do not understand my own actions. For I do not do what I want, but I do the very thing I hate" (Rom 7:14–15).

Don't be so stubborn that you can't give up some destructive habit. It can be fatal. Consider the story of a man who one day took a canoe trip with his dad and sons. By afternoon they were out on the lake fishing. Suddenly, the grandfather's rod bent double, and the kids were celebrating. One boy held the dip net as his grandfather slowly brought the fish in. The catch suddenly shot up from the water. There was a hooked fourteen-inch walleye in the mouth of a thirty-five-inch northern pike! They got the net under them and caught both. That big fish became dinner because he was too stubborn to let go of the little fish!

Are we like that? Do we hold on to something out of stubbornness until we destroy our lives? The gospel says it possible to leave our destructive habits behind. God promises freedom and autonomy: "We know that our old self was crucified with him so that the body of sin might be destroyed, and we might no longer be enslaved to sin. For sin will have no dominion over you, since you are not under law but under grace" (Rom 6:6, 14).

So let's leave our destructive habits behind us and get on with our lives.

Yes, there are things we need to leave behind. We can become transformed people if we are able to break the fatal chain of negative traits and actions that have been passed down for generations. We can affect many lives for good. Sometimes we get stuck between two worlds: the one of the past that we need to release and the one of the future we are reluctant to enter. But Jesus said, "you will know the truth, and the truth will make you free" (John 8:32).

If an old memory still hurts, then we haven't left it behind. Paul said, "So if anyone is in Christ, there is a new creation: everything old has passed away; see, everything has become new!" (2 Cor 5:17).

Easter

The Victory of Easter
John 16:7, 28, 32-33; 1 John 4:4

For Christians, Easter is a day of celebration, a proclamation of triumph, a declaration of victory. Jesus himself expressed its significance by saying, "I have said this to you, so that in me you may have peace. In the world you face persecution. But take courage; I have conquered the world!" (John 16:33).

Later, John includes us in that promise, saying, "Whatever is born of God conquers the world. And this is the victory that conquers the world, our faith" (1 John 5:4).

It's encouraging to know that God can love us at our worst, before we reform. The prodigal son was not told he had to reform before he could be accepted. He was not forced to apologize. He was not punished for his sin, because he had already been punished by his sin.

Jacob was a liar, but he wasn't held to his past. Zacchaeus was a thief, but he wasn't held to his past. Paul was a murderer, but he wasn't held to his past. Neither are we!

This love and acceptance is complete and permanent. It's not contingent on anything we think, say, or do. Since we have this assurance, we can acknowledge our negative attitudes, our selfish ambitions, and our immature reactions. We can admit our sins. We can be honest.

As human beings we have many problems that hinder and harm us. Jesus lived and died to help us overcome these destructive things. He said, "Just as the Son of Man came not to be served but to serve, and to give his life a ransom for many" (Matt 20:28).

What are our greatest weaknesses and burdens?

I. We Have Feelings of Shame and Guilt.

President Truman said, "The buck stops here!" For some of us, however, not only our buck, but everybody else's bucks seem to stop here! Over the years some of us take on the problems of the world. We assume responsibility for our relatives and acquaintances. We feel guilty if anyone anywhere fails at anything.

Because we're insecure, we punish ourselves with criticism and condemnation. We push ourselves to be "all things to all people." We fragment ourselves in order to give little pieces of our time and energy to everyone who needs us.

Inevitably, we finally begin to burn out and become bitter. We still serve, but we do it reluctantly and out of a sense of duty. Furthermore, we lose ourselves in the process. In fact, the whole thing is futile. One person can't meet every need and fulfill every desire. If we're real and honest and open, then we can be God's partners, but we can't be God. So some bucks should stop here, but others must be sent on their way. If the bucks pile up, so does the guilt.

Guilt that motivates us when we shirk our responsibility can be productive, but guilt for events beyond our control is a sin! Scripture says, "If we confess our sins, he who is faithful and just will forgive us our sins and cleanse us from all unrighteousness" (1 John 1:9).

God removes unproductive shame and guilt, and that's the victory of Easter.

II. We Have Feelings of Anxiety and Fear.

Fortunately, Jesus did not bring a negative message. He didn't give a list of rules and regulations. He didn't issue a lot of taboos and threats. He didn't criticize or condemn sinners.

Instead, Jesus offered total acceptance: "Everything that the Father gives me will come to me, and anyone who comes to me I will never drive away" (John 6:37).

Jesus offered unconditional love: "No one has greater love than this, to lay down one's life for one's friends" (John 15:13).

Jesus offered infinite value: "So do not be afraid; you are of more value than many sparrows" (Matt 10:31).

Jesus offered absolute security: "I am with you always, to the end of the age" (Matt 28:20).

Jesus offered eternal hope: "All things can be done for the one who believes" (Mark 9:23).

These are the deep psychological assurances that can change us, fulfill us, and empower us. The gospel lowers the proud and raises the humble. It shows the vulnerability of the strong and gives strength to the weak. It reminds us that the ground is level at the foot of the cross.

When a sinner realizes that he has infinite worth and has an absolute assurance of God's presence, he experiences a great liberation. The good news of the gospel helps us realize that it's okay to make mistakes; it's okay to fail; it's okay to be a human being. Jesus said, "Peace I leave with you; my peace I give to you. I do not give to you as the world gives. Do not let your hearts be troubled, and do not let them be afraid" (John 14:27).

These words abolish anxiety and fear, and that's the victory of Easter.

III. We Have Feelings of Rage and Resentment.

One of the hardest lessons we must learn is that life isn't always fair. Over and over, we're told that if we do good things, we receive good things; if we do bad things, we receive bad things. But that's not always true. If we do good things and then receive bad things, this causes us to have doubts and anger.

Jesus tries to help us face reality. In fact, he says the opposite: "Blessed are those who are persecuted for righteousness' sake, for theirs is the kingdom of heaven" (Matt 5:10).

Furthermore, he says God is even-handed: "He makes his sun rise on the evil and on the good, and sends rain on the righteous and on the unrighteous" (Matt 5:45).

In fact, the crucifixion stands forever as a symbol of the unfairness of life. The best person received the worst treatment. The innocent Jesus is killed, and the guilty Barabbas goes free. It's not fair!

Yes, life is tilted toward progress, but that doesn't ensure fairness in every situation. However, we do have the assurance that, ultimately, truth will triumph. Scripture says, "Little children, you are from God, and have conquered them; for the one who is in you is greater than the one who is in the world" (1 John 4:4).

Trusting that justice will ultimately prevail allows us to let go of rage and resentment, and that's the victory of Easter.

According to legend, a young woman sat down on a park bench and dropped a large bag at her feet. She had been carrying it so long that her arms ached and her back was stiff. Oh, to be rid of this load of garbage.

She used to peek into the bag, but what she saw repelled her, so she's kept it closed ever since. There was no one to help her carry it because everyone else had their own load.

As she rested for a moment, she saw a mother leading a child with one hand and dragging a trash bag heavy with guilt. She hadn't been a good parent. Then a very old man passed. His trash bag was so long that it hit the back of his legs. It was filled with regrets. He had neglected his family, and his children hated him.

A car stopped, and a man got out, pulling a bag lumpy with resentments. He draped it over his shoulder and cursed the weight.

A teenage girl walked by mumbling, "Rage! That's what I'm carrying. Rage at my parents. But I'm tired of this anger. He said he'd take it." She motioned to her bag: "So I'm going to give it to him."

Then the woman on the bench saw others who seemed to be walking in the same direction. One tramp smelled of alcohol. He'd slept in his clothes. Another was an ex-con with numerous crimes in his past.

The woman decided to follow and see where these burdened people were going. Finally, she saw a man with a kind smile and open arms. As each person approached, he reached out and said, "May I take your burden, and may you never carry it again."

When it was her turn, the woman hesitated, but his eyes drew her forward. Then she heard those gentle words: "You have a bag of shame, too many wrong partners and too many wrong choices." She braced herself for the scorn she expected to hear. She awaited judgment, but it never came. Instead, his voice was warm, his question personal: "Will you give me your trash?"

"You can't live with this," he explained. "You weren't made to bear such burdens."

"Come to me, all you that are weary and are carrying heavy burdens, and I will give you rest" (Matt 11:28).

This is the universal story. This is our story. We all have trash. We all have garbage. We all have shame, guilt, anxiety, fear, rage, and resentment. We all have regrets, mistakes, problems, and weaknesses. Scripture says, "All have sinned and fall short of the glory of God" (Rom 3:23).

The wonderful promise of the gospel is that we don't have to carry our loads of shame and guilt. We don't have to carry our loads of anxiety and fear. We don't have to carry our loads of rage and resentment. Jesus took them away forever!

That's the victory of Easter!

Losers Who Win!

In 2004 an Olympic athlete lost every individual race in the decathlon and yet won the gold medal. During the American Revolution, George Washington lost almost every battle, yet he won the war. After the crucifixion, Jesus's disciples thought all was lost, and most of them went back to their former occupations. The women who came to the tomb thought all was lost and were prepared to arrange Jesus's broken body. Judas, who had betrayed the Lord, thought all was lost and killed himself.

The enemies of Jesus thought they had won. This man who had challenged their teachings, changed their traditions, and flaunted their rules and regulations was dead and they were safe. Things could remain the way they'd always been.

Three days later, everything had changed. The world looked completely different. All was not lost! Good had overcome evil! Truth had triumphed over falsehood! The tomb was empty! Life had conquered death, and victory was declared! Things were not the way they had always been. Indeed, things were so radically different that life would never be the same again.

That's why we celebrate Easter. For Peter, Easter was a life-changing event. Things were never the same again. Before, he had lied, cursed, and denied the Lord. Afterward, he preached to thousands, supported the church, and was willing to die for his faith. Peter was a loser who won!

Easter is a life-changing event. Today, most people may not be aware of the many changes and positive effects of Easter, but they are all around us. When slaves are freed, when Jews are liberated from Nazi death camps, when democracies flourish, we remember that Jesus said, "The Spirit of the Lord is upon me, because he has anointed me to bring good news to the poor. He has sent me to proclaim release to the captives...to let the oppressed go free" (Luke 4:18).

And "if the Son makes you free, you will be free indeed" (John 8:36). Easter turns losers into winners!

When the Red Cross ministers to hurricane victims, when there are food drops for starving people, when senior citizens get Meals on Wheels, we remember that Jesus said, "Just as you did it to one of the least of these who are members of my family, you did it to me." (Matt 25:40). Easter turns losers into winners!

When an alcoholic recovers, when a blind man has cataract surgery, when a cancer is put into remission, we remember that Jesus said, "The one who believes in me will also do the works that I do and, in fact, will do greater works than these" (John 14:12). Easter turns losers into winners!

When children are fed and nurtured, we remember that Jesus said, "Whoever gives even a cup of cold water to one of these little ones...truly I tell you, none of these will lose their reward" (Matt 10:42). Easter turns losers into winners!

When child abuse is prevented, we remember that Jesus said, "If any of you put a stumbling block before one of these little ones who believe in me, it would be better for you if a great millstone were fastened around your neck and you were drowned in the depth of the sea" (Matt 18:6). Easter turns losers into winners!

When women are allowed to vote and enjoy equal rights with men, we remember that Jesus defended Mary when she chose to learn rather than serve in the kitchen. He said, "Mary has chosen the better part, which will not be taken away from her" (Luke 10:42). Easter turns losers into winners!

When volunteers for Habitat for Humanity provide shelter for the needy, we remember that Jesus said, "Let your light shine before others, so that they may see your good works and give glory to your Father in heaven" (Matt 5:16). Easter turns losers into winners!

When illiterates are taught to read, we remember that Jesus "had compassion for them, because they were like sheep without a shepherd; and he began to teach them many things" (Mark 6:34). Easter turns losers into winners!

When people receive grief counseling, when scientists discover healing medicines, when inventors develop safety devices, we are blessed. Easter turns losers into winners!

In fact, all of the social progress and educational advances and humane improvements of the last 2,000 years are the direct results of Jesus's life, death, and resurrection. Easter turns losers into winners!

For each of us as Christians, Easter is certainly a life-changing event. It's the ultimate promise of success! It gives us the absolute assurance of victory. No matter if there are long days and dark nights, no matter if there are disappointments and tragedies, no matter if there are failures and lost battles, we know that in the end there is victory!

Once, some fans were watching their favorite football team play in the Super Bowl. They had been out of the country and missed the actual game, so this was a rerun. They were glued to the TV. As they saw fumbles and missed touchdown opportunities, the groans and miserable faces had created a dismal atmosphere for the entire first half. Just then, another fan wandered in and said, "What's the matter, guys? Why are you so upset? I saw this game. I know the final score. Don't despair! These are just minor setbacks. When we reach the last quarter, you'll see; we will win!"

So, Christians, remember this: God has seen this game. He knows the final score. Don't despair! Our problems and distresses are just minor setbacks. When we reach the last quarter, you'll see; we will win!

Easter turns losers into winners!

Where Is the Risen Christ?

Matthew 28:18-20

God is with us. That is the message of Easter. The risen Christ said, "Remember, I am with you always, to the very end of the age." This promise is repeated over and over again in the scriptures:

The risen Christ appeared to Mary in the garden, giving her the good news she needed.

He appeared dramatically to the disciples in the upper room, giving them the encouragement they needed.

He appeared again to doubting Thomas, giving him the assurance he needed.

He appeared to those two disillusioned men on the Emmaus road, giving them the hope they needed.

He appeared to Simon Peter on the seashore, giving him the forgiveness he so desperately needed.

Then, there is his promise to us: "I am with you always, to the end of the age" (Matt 28:20b).

A few years ago, a schoolteacher asked her pupils, "Who is the greatest living person?" Some wrote the name of a president; some wrote "Billy Graham"; some wrote the names of other prominent people of our time. But one little girl wrote "Jesus."

Noting this last answer, the teacher explained, "Honey, I said 'the greatest living person.'"

"But he is living," the little girl insisted.

The Easter message says, "Jesus Christ is alive today!" But many "believers" are not sure just where he is.

Once, two children were studying a portrait of Queen Victoria on her throne. "What's she doing?" one of them asked. The other gazed at the picture and said, "Oh, she's not doing anything. She's just sitting there reigning."

Is that our view of Jesus? Do we think he is just sitting upon a celestial throne, far removed from the problems of the world? Is he just sitting there reigning? This is not scriptural. This is not the gospel. This is not the good news of Easter. Jesus said, "I am with you always." What does that mean? Where can his presence be felt?

I. We Can Find the Risen Christ Wherever His People Are Hurting.

It seems more reasonable to find the Lord in the beautiful, sacred places of the earth, or in those high moments when everything is going our way. But the truth is that the risen Christ is never nearer to us than when we are hurting.

In the Gospels we find him with the poor, the lame, the blind, the sick, and the hungry.

It's the same today. We feel his presence with us when we're hurting, because we are more open to him. We are more willing for him to come and help us. God is like a loving parent, and all good, loving parents want to be with their children when they are hurting. David said, "The LORD is a stronghold for the oppressed, a stronghold in times of trouble" (Ps 9:9).

Once, a preacher was at a hospital visiting a little girl who was very sick. Her mother had been at her bedside for several days. The doctor said, "Preacher, see if you can get that lady to go home for a while. She hasn't slept, she hasn't eaten, and she's got to be exhausted.

The preacher touched the woman's arm and said, "Why don't you let me take you home for a little while?"

She looked up and spoke through her tears, "You don't really expect me to leave my child when she is so sick, do you?

God is like that—a loving parent who wants to be especially close to his children when they are hurting.

II. We Can Find the Risen Christ Wherever His People Are Serving.

Before the ascension, Jesus gave us a job. He told us to go out into the world, preaching and teaching and serving. And then he added that great promise: "Remember, I am with you always."

After sixteen very difficult years of service as a missionary in the heart of Africa, David Livingstone returned to his native land of Scotland. During his furlough he was asked to speak to the students at Glasgow University. His body was weakened from his experience. In Africa he suffered and survived twenty-seven bouts with tropical fever. One of his arms hung motionless at his side, the result of being mangled by a lion. As he stood before those students at the university, he said, "I will tell you what sustained me amidst the toil, the hardship, the suffering and the loneliness. It was Christ's promise, 'I am with you always'" (Matt 28:20).

One of the most convincing proofs of a living Christ is the unselfish service of his people. Jesus said, "For I was hungry and you gave me food, I was thirsty and you gave me something to drink, I was a stranger and you welcomed me, I was naked and you gave me clothing, I was sick and you took care of me, I was in prison and you visited me. ...Truly I tell you, just as you did it to one of the least of these who are members of my family, you did it to me." (Matt 25:35–36, 40).

We never feel a greater consciousness of the Lord's presence than when we are sharing our faith and our love with others.

Wherever people are working, helping, healing, and serving, the risen Lord is there.

III. We Can Find the Risen Christ Wherever His People Are Worshiping.

Jesus said, "For where two or three are gathered in my name, I am there among them" (Matt 18:20).

The phone rang in the office of a Washington church one Sunday morning. The voice asked, "Will the president be in church today?" The pastor replied, "I'm not sure, but I do know this: Jesus Christ will be here, and that should be enough incentive for you to come."

Once, when the Queen of England toured Canada, she attended a little church in Niagara Falls. People jammed the auditorium and filled the church lawn with the hope of getting a glimpse of the queen. Jesus Christ, the king of kings, has promised to attend every service where even two or three gather in his name, yet we take that promise lightly. We only make it to church when it's convenient. We only make it to church if we can work it into our busy schedule.

One of the best places to feel the Lord's presence is in his church. He said, "On this rock I will build my church, and the gates of Hades will not prevail against it" (Matt 16:18).

Wherever people are worshiping, the risen Christ is there.

So we can find the risen Lord wherever his people are hurting, wherever his people are serving, and wherever his people are worshiping.

That's the message of Easter.

In one of history's most decisive battles, Wellington was locked in combat with Napoleon at Waterloo. News of the final result could not come back to

London by radio or telegraph; neither had been invented yet. All England waited breathlessly as news was relayed by semaphore signals.

From the top of Winchester Cathedral, a semaphore began to spell out the message, letter by letter: "Wellington defeated." At this moment a dense fog settled in and obliterated the flashing light. Those two words shrouded Londoners with despair. All was lost.

But when the mist lifted, the signaler sent his message again, just to be sure it got through. It said, "Wellington defeated the enemy." What a difference those two extra words made. Gloom became gladness. England was safe. The future was secure.

Similar reversals appear between the Saturday and Sunday of that first Easter. Saturday, the message was bleak: "Jesus defeated. Our master is dead and buried. A stone seals his body in a tomb. It's all over."

But Sunday morning brought a new phrase: Jesus defeated death! "He is risen! What he taught is true! Christ lives!"

One of the greatest messages of Easter is that "God is with us." Paul said, "In him we live and move and have our being" (Acts 17:28).

The risen Christ is not sitting on a far-off throne reigning. He is here! He is among us! He is in our hearts and lives.

The Demands of Easter

Mark 8:34-35

Easter is a joyful occasion. We talk about the benefits of salvation, the blessings of discipleship, and the advantages of being a Christian. There is another side to this, however, and to be absolutely honest, we must present it.

Jesus himself emphasized the requirements and became an example of the consequences as he went to the cross. He said devotion costs: "If any want to become my followers, let them deny themselves and take up their cross and follow me" (Mark 8:34).

As Christians we have to be better than average. As Christians we must outlive the ordinary person. As Christians we can't just continue doing what feels good. More is expected of us. Jesus said, "From everyone to whom much has been given, much will be required" (Luke 12:48).

So what are the demands of Easter?

I. Selfishness Is Out.

It's normal to be selfish. But as Christians we no longer have that option. Jesus said, "I seek to do not my own will but the will of him who sent me" (John 5:30).

Looking out for "number one" may be human nature. Self-preservation may be based on instinct. Nevertheless, as Christians we must have higher ideals. John said, "He laid down his life for us—and we ought to lay down our lives for one another" (1 John 3:16).

As Christians we can't choose our occupations by income alone. We can't vote our pocketbooks. We can't feather our own nests at the expense of others. Selfishness is out! Jesus said, "No one has greater love than this, to lay down one's life for one's friends" (John 15:13). And he did that.

Paul said, "[Jesus] gave himself for our sins" (Gal 1:4).

Therefore, as Christians we must give ourselves up for others. That's one of the demands of Easter.

II. Defensiveness Is Out.

It's normal to be defensive, but as Christians we no longer have that option. Jesus said, "Do not resist an evildoer" (Matt 5:39).

Paul said, "See that none of you repays evil for evil, but always seek to do good to one another and to all" (1 Thess 5:15).

Too many of us are like the porcupine. This defensive animal uses its needle-sharp quills in reaction to threats. Other animals yield out of fear, not respect. It may be true that the porcupine is never kicked, but it's never hugged either!

Yes, it's natural to be defensive. Lashing out and hitting back may be automatic responses. Protecting ourselves and blaming others may be normal behavior. Nevertheless, as Christians we must be different.

Paul said, "Beloved, never avenge yourselves... Do not be overcome by evil, but overcome evil with good" (Rom 12:19a, 21).

Once, a native guide accompanied a missionary on a trip, but he refused to accept the gospel. On the way, they had car trouble and tried to wave down a passing truck, but it refused to stop. Finally, the missionary got the car started, and they continued on their way, but they had not gone far when they came upon a stalled truck with the two men who had failed to help them. The native laughed, "Now we can pay those fellows back. They passed us up, and we'll pass them up." "Oh, no," the missionary said. "We must stop and help them."

Afterward, the native said to the missionary, "Sir, now I understand. Your gospel is about a Christ who came to help not only his friends, but his enemies."

Yes, forgiveness is required. Defensiveness is out. Jesus was not defensive, even against those who crucified him. He said, "Father, forgive them; for they do not know what they are doing" (Luke 23:34).

We must do likewise! That's another demand of Easter.

III. Mediocrity Is Out.

It's normal to just get by and take the easy road. But as Christians we no longer have that option. Paul said, "Do not lag in zeal, be ardent in spirit, serve the Lord" (Rom 12:10–11).

Being "average" if you can be better is sinful. Once, some of Teddy Roosevelt's supporters called him an "extraordinary man." When the president heard them, he said, "Oh, no. I'm not an extraordinary man. I'm just a plain, ordinary man, highly motivated."

Yes, it's natural to be mediocre. Inertia is a principle of the physical world. Even water runs downhill. Laziness is a constant temptation of mankind. Nevertheless, as Christians we must overcome these tendencies.

As Christians we can't be clock watchers. We can't give the least effort for the most returns. The needs are great! Excellence is in! Mediocrity is out. Jesus said, "Whoever does not carry the cross and follow me cannot be my disciple" (Luke 14:27).

That's another demand of Easter! Being a Christian requires our best in love, forgiveness, and service. We may emphasize the benefits of salvation, the blessings of discipleship, and the advantages of being a Christian, but Jesus also emphasized the opposite. He warned of hardships and obligations. He was honest about the demands of being a Christian. He said, "If any want to become my followers, let them deny themselves and take up their cross and follow me. For those who want to save their life will lose it, and those who lose their life for my sake, and for the sake of the gospel, will save it" (Mark 8:34–35).

God expects great things of us. We have enormous responsibilities. We are here for a purpose. Paul said, "You are not your own... For you were bought with a price; therefore glorify God in your body" (1 Cor 6:19–20).

We celebrate Easter because Jesus paid that price!

A Japanese missionary was going home one night when he saw a person jump in the river. The missionary dragged him out, took him home, nursed him back to health, and found him a job.

Then he said, "Remember this: From now on, your life no longer belongs to you. I saved it, so it belongs to me. Therefore, you must report to me regularly on what you've been doing with 'my life.'"

Surprisingly, the man had a successful life. Years later, he asked his benefactor this question: "I know you saved me from death, but where did you get the notion that my life no longer belongs to me?"

"That's not a notion," the missionary replied. "That's the truth. In fact, my life doesn't really belong to me. It was given to me by God, and I must stand before him and tell him what I've done with it!"

In stating the theme of the Easter message, Paul said, "He died for all, so that those who live might live no longer for themselves, but for him who died and was raised for them" (2 Cor 5:15).

So this Easter morning is a time for us to celebrate the Lord's death, burial, and resurrection, but it's also a time for us to go forth and live the marvelous resurrection life God has given us!

The Lessons of Easter

On Easter we usually emphasize the death, burial, and resurrection of Jesus. But how can we understand and apply these events in our lives today? What are the lessons of Easter?

I. Easter Assures Us That Truth Will Triumph Over Falsehood!

Jesus said, "You will know the truth, and the truth will make you free" (John 8:32). A famous quotation expresses it this way: "Truth crushed to earth shall rise again." Both of these statements tell us that lies and deceit are self-defeating.

Jesus lived and died for truth. When he came before Pilate, Jesus said, "For this I was born, and for this I came into the world, to testify to the truth. Everyone who belongs to the truth listens to my voice" (John 18:37). Truth is so important that Jesus prayed for us that we may know truth, saying, "Sanctify them in the truth; your word is truth" (John 17:17). Paul also emphasized truth, saying, "[God] desires everyone to be saved and to come to the knowledge of the truth" (1 Tim 2:4).

Jesus's death, burial, and resurrection demonstrate this principle. They are proof that truth will triumph!

II. Easter Assures Us That Good Is More Powerful Than Evil!

Peter said, "Do not repay evil for evil or abuse for abuse; but, on the contrary, repay with a blessing. It is for this that you were called—that you might inherit a blessing. Now who will harm you if you are eager to do what is good?" (1 Pet 3:9, 13). This scripture shows us that two wrongs don't make a right; an "eye for an eye" mentality only results in total blindness. You can't fight evil with evil. Jesus said, "You have heard that it was said, 'You shall love your neighbor and hate your enemy.' But I say to you, Love your enemies and pray for those who persecute you, so that you may be children of your Father in heaven; for he makes his sun rise on the evil and on the good, and sends rain on the righteous and on the unrighteous" (Matt 5:43–45).

Paul explains this very clearly when he says, "See that none of you repays evil for evil, but always seek to do good to one another and to all" (1 Thess 5:15). Then he tells us how to do this, saying, "Do not be overcome by evil, but overcome evil with good" (Rom 12:21).

Jesus's death, burial, and resurrection demonstrate this principle. They are proof that good is more powerful than evil.

III. Easter Assures Us That Victory Is More Certain Than Defeat!

Jesus said, "I have said this to you, so that in me you may have peace. In the world you face persecution. But take courage; I have conquered the world!" (John 16:33).

When Jesus prayed in the garden of Gethsemane and said, "Not my will, but thine be done," he was saying, "God's will and purpose for the overall benefit of mankind is more important than my own personal desires" (see Matt 26). At that moment he won the battle with evil.

When Jesus honored the thief on the cross who asked for mercy by promising him paradise instead of giving him criticism and condemnation, he won the battle with evil.

When Jesus forgave the soldiers who crucified him, rather than demanding justice or plotting revenge, he won the battle with evil.

John said, "Because you know the Father...because...the word of God abides in you...you have overcome the evil one" (1 John 2:14).

"Little children, you are from God, and have conquered them; for the one who is in you is greater than the one who is in the world" (1 John 4:4).

"Whatever is born of God conquers the world. And this is the victory that conquers the world, our faith" (1 John 5:4–5).

The writer of Revelation said, "To everyone who conquers, I will give permission to eat from the tree of life that is in the paradise of God" (Rev 2:7).

"I am the Alpha and the Omega, the beginning and the end... Those who conquer will inherit these things, and I will be their God and they will be my children" (Rev 21:6–7).

As Christians we are on the winning side. Jesus's death, burial, and resurrection demonstrate this principle. They are proof that victory is more certain than defeat!

So the lessons of Easter teach us to avoid falsehood and trust in truth. They help us to overcome evil by promoting good. They tell us we won't suffer defeat because victory is assured! The lessons of Easter give us hope!

Yes, there is both truth and falsehood in this world. Yes, we experience both good and evil in this world. Yes, we face the possibility of either victory or defeat in this world. But Easter prepares us to make wise choices.

Easter fortifies us in our battles. Easter assures us of ultimate success. Paul said, "Indeed, we live as human beings, but we do not wage war according to human standards; for the weapons of our warfare are not merely human, but they have divine power to destroy strongholds. We destroy arguments and every proud obstacle raised up against the knowledge of God, and we take every thought captive to obey Christ" (2 Cor 10:3–5).

"May the God of hope fill you with all joy and peace in believing, so that you may abound in hope by the power of the Holy Spirit" (Rom 15:13).

Truth will triumph! Goodness will prevail! Victory is assured! Those are the lessons of Easter.

Mother's Day

Pointers for Parents
Ephesians 6:1-4

The psalmist said, "[Children] are indeed a heritage from the Lord, the fruit of the womb a reward" (Ps 127:3). That's true, but children are also an awesome responsibility. Once, an exasperated mother was asked, "If you had to do it over, would you have children? "Oh, sure!" she said after a pause. "Just not the same ones!"

We've all felt like that at times. One mother compiled what she called the five most useful sentences for parents:
1. Where's your other shoe?
2. Give that back to your sister.
3. Don't play with your food.
4. Who did that?
5. Take that thing out of your mouth!

An old proverb says, "God couldn't be everywhere, so he made mothers." But sometimes it's hard to live up to such standards. One mother wrote, "I challenge any woman to feel good about herself after yelling at her eight-year-old all the way to school because she had to drive him while wearing her bathrobe. She had to drive because he was late. He was late because at 7:30 that morning, he remembered that he had promised the teacher he would bring two dozen homemade cookies for a party. The trip to school involved angry words from a mom, two tears trickling down a child's face, and a screeching stop at a bakery."

Yes, parenting is hard, but let's look at "The Three Ls of Parenting."

I. We Must Love Our Children.

We must love them unconditionally—not for something or because of something. There must be no "ifs" or "buts" or "maybes." This kind of love means to give children respect, appreciation, attention, and praise. It means to listen to them, hug them, and value them.

We must provide what they need, not necessarily what they want. Paul said, "Let love be genuine; hate what is evil, hold fast to what is good" (Rom 12:9).

Sometimes when a child has misbehaved, parents think they don't deserve love and attention, but just the opposite is true. Children actually need love most when they deserve it least. How can we teach them of God's love and grace if we only accept them when they are good?

Too often, parents use children for their own egos. One woman said, "I wanted my girls to have good manners and make good grades so people would see what a wonderful mother I was. I had to learn to want what was best for them, rather than what would satisfy my pride."

A good parent views the child as a person, not as a possession. One TV journalist said, "In trying to combine a career and a family, I wasn't always successful, but my daughter is great today, and I think it was because every time she called, I took the call, even if I was with the president of the United States or the queen of England."

Our kids need to be our first priority, and they need to know they're our first priority. Giving love is essential.

II. We Must Limit Our Children.

Limits give security, like a bannister on a balcony or a fence around the yard. But our demands and rules should be about major things, not minor things. That means we must be strict on safety and moral issues and not so strict on fads and customs.

Things like drunk driving and honesty are majors. Things like t-shirts and hairstyles are minors. Also, let them have their say even if you can't let them have their way. Allowing them to express their feelings is very important.

Solomon said, "Train children in the right way, and when old, they will not stray" (Prov 22:6). This means to instruct and guide. To do this, make sure the limits are clear and specific. Make sure there are consequences for ignoring the limits, and make sure you notice and praise them when they keep within the limits. A counselor said, "You can't expect a child to walk a thin line. No one can! Instead, you should establish two boundaries and then give the child a little space in between."

He also suggested widening the boundaries if a child does well, but tightening them if the child does poorly. Some youngsters can walk successfully within mile-wide boundaries while others can only handle six-inch-wide boundaries.

Setting limits is essential.

III. We Must Lead Our Children.

We lead by example. We show with our life. We demonstrate with our deeds. Children will do what we do, not necessarily what we say. Paul said, "Set the believers an example in speech and conduct, in love, in faith, in purity" (1 Tim 4:12).

Statistics indicate that most children are visual learners. They learn from copying what they see. It's our responsibility to show them a living faith. Paul described this to Timothy by saying, "From childhood you have known the sacred writings that are able to instruct you for salvation through faith in Christ Jesus" (2 Tim 3:15).

As parents we often hope our boys and girls will learn Scripture in Sunday school. But just memorizing Bible verses is not enough. A child may be able to repeat the words to hundreds of verses and still not know their true meaning. We must show our children how to apply the verses by putting them into practice. Then we must be committed church members. The writer of Hebrews said, "[Let us not neglect] to meet together…but [let us encourage] one another" (Heb 10:25).

We shouldn't attend church only when we feel like it. Children decide what's important by observing our actions. They notice that we go to work in bad weather, but we don't go to church if it's raining. We make them attend school even if they're sleepy after a late night out, but we don't make them attend church after a late night out. Remember, Jesus said, "Strive first for the kingdom of God and his righteousness" (Matt 6:33).

Above all, we must set moral standards. Paul says, "Abstain from every form of evil" (1 Thess 5:22). This is hard in today's world. Parents watch inappropriate movies, gossip about their neighbors, yell at the umpire during a little league game. Kids watch these actions. The old saying "Do as I say and not as I do" doesn't work. The things you do as a parent now are the things your children are likely to do for the rest of their lives.

Leading by example is essential.

Yes, the psalmist said, "[Children] are indeed a heritage of the LORD" (Ps 127:3).

An old legend expresses it well: Once upon a time, when a baby was ready to be born, it said, "God, they say today you are sending me to earth, but I'm so small and helpless. How am I going to live there?"

God answered, "I have chosen a special angel just for you. She is waiting to take care of you."

"But," the baby persisted, "here in heaven I sing and smile, and that makes me happy."

"Well, your angel will sing and smile. You will feel your angel's love and be happy."

"What am I going to do when I want to talk to you?"

"Your angel will teach you how to pray!"

"But I've heard there are bad people on earth. Who will protect me?"

"Your angel will risk her own life to defend you."

At that moment there was a silence in heaven, and voices from earth could already be heard. The child hurriedly whispered, "Oh, God, if I'm about to leave, please tell me my angel's name."

God smiled and said, "My child, your angel's name is not important, because you will always call her 'Mother'!"

This is Mother's Day. It's a day to honor parents and cherish children. It's a day to dedicate ourselves to our families.

Love them!

Limit them!

Lead them!

The ABCs of Parenting
Matthew 18:1-6

Scripture says, "[Children] are indeed a heritage from the LORD" (Ps 127:3). It also says, "Train children in the right way, and when old, they will not stray" (Prov 22:6).

Jesus valued children and gave severe warnings about their abuse or neglect. According to Scripture "the disciples came to Jesus and asked, 'Who is the greatest in the kingdom of heaven?' He called a child, whom he put among them, and said, 'Truly I tell you, unless you change and become like children, you will never enter the kingdom of heaven. Whoever becomes humble like this child is the greatest in the kingdom of heaven. Whoever welcomes one such child in my name welcomes me. If any of you put a stumbling block before one of these little ones who believe in me, it would be better for you if a great millstone were fastened around your neck and you were drowned in the depth of the sea'" (Matt 18:1–6).

Yes, children are important. Let's look at the ABCs of parenting:

A. Accept children as they are. Don't force them into your image. Let them have their own personality, even if it's different from yours.
B. Believe in each child's potential. We must respect the youth of today. Children have enormous possibilities for either good or evil. So much depends upon how they're trained and taught.
C. Criticize sparingly and constructively. Harsh criticism is hurtful, and hurting a child has serious consequences. Paul said, "Put away from you all bitterness and wrath and anger and wrangling and slander, together with all malice" (Eph 4:31).
D. Discover your children's special talents.
E. Encourage them to use their gifts and abilities. Enjoy their spontaneity and creativity. Scripture says, "Remember your creator in the days of your youth, before the days of trouble come, and the years draw near when you will say, 'I have no pleasure in them'" (Eccl 12:1).
F. Focus on strengths, not weaknesses. Jesus looked at the religious leaders of his day and called them "a generation of vipers." But he looked at the children and said, "Of such is the kingdom of Heaven."

G. Give unconditional love. There is no substitute for love! Good mothers provide unconditional love.
H. Hear what your child has to say. Most parents talk more than they listen. Try to hear and understand your children's opinions and concerns.
I. Ignore unimportant mistakes. Parents tend to point out the failures and overlook the successes. Once, two kids were fighting when their mother yelled, "Why can't you two ever get along and play quietly?" "Oh, we do!" the children replied. "But when we do that, you don't notice."
J. Join in their activities. Families need happy traditions and positive customs. Times together are important. Birthdays, graduations, and holiday celebrations give us opportunities to make memories.
K. Keep children away from evil. Provide a safe environment and healthy activities.
L. Let them have their say, even if you can't let them have their way.
M. Make the most of their individuality. You can't treat every boy and girl the same. Scripture says, "Train each child in the way he should go."
N. Nurture them in spiritual areas. Children will usually follow in their parents' footsteps. Your children need to see you active in church, in prayer, and in Bible reading.
O. Offer total forgiveness. Don't keep remembering and emphasizing their past mistakes and failures.
P. Praise regularly and productively. Paul said, "Therefore encourage one another and build up each other" (1 Thess 5:11a).
Q. Question children about their goals and dreams. Remind them that God has a plan for their lives.
R. Respect their viewpoint. They don't have to agree with you on everything.
S. Satisfy their need for security. Children may rebel against restrictions, but they need boundaries and will appreciate guidelines.
T. Take time to touch. Jesus held the little children and put his hands on them. Touching is essential.
U. Understand their problems. The young age presents the most teachable moments. Example is the best teacher.
V. Value their ideas and suggestions. Children need to feel their parents' approval. Honest discussion and conversation are important.

W. Warn them about life's pitfalls. Jesus said, "Stay awake and pray that you may not come into the time of trial; the spirit indeed is willing, but the flesh is weak" (Matt 26:41).

X. Exercise patience and kindness. Responsible parents have empathy and concern. A mother's patience is like a tube of toothpaste; you can always squeeze out just a little bit more.

Y. Yield control as soon as responsibility develops. Let children make their own decisions as often as possible.

Z. Zealously defend their right to autonomy. Each child is unique.

Mamie Gene Cole expressed it this way in poetry:

> I am the child.
> You hold in your hand my destiny.
> Give me, I pray you, those things that make for success.
> Train me, I beg you, That I may be a blessing to the world.

In the eleventh century, Duke Robert of Burgundy was a great warrior. Once, just before he departed on a campaign, he made his barons and nobles come and swear allegiance to his baby boy just in case something happened to him. They came with clanking armor and knelt before the little boy.

One baron smiled as he bowed. "The child is so little," he remarked.

"Yes, he is little," said the duke, "but he will grow."

Indeed, he did grow. That baby became known as William the Conqueror of England.

Our children may be little now, but they will grow! They may seem insignificant now, but that will change! Helping these little ones find and fulfill their God-given potential is at the heart of the gospel. We must make the most of our brief time with them. Teaching and influencing our children is the most important thing we will ever do!

Changing the Course of History

If I could tell you how to double your income this year, would you listen? Of course you would!

If I could tell you how to improve your gas mileage by fifty percent, would you listen? Of course you would!

If I could tell you how to cut your grocery bill in half, would you listen? Of course you would!

But if I could tell you how you can change the course of world history, would you listen?

Well, you might not listen because you probably wouldn't believe you could do that. But nearly everyone here today is in a position to change the future of history. How can you do that? You can do it by being a godly parent!

There's no greater responsibility than that of being a parent. The child you shape today will change the world of tomorrow. Yes, the kind of parent you are can change world history by making it worse! Adolf Hitler was once an innocent baby with parents. But he changed world history by becoming a ruthless killer. Lee Harvey Oswald was once an innocent baby with parents. But he changed world history by assassinating a president.

On the other hand, the kind of parents you are can change world history by making it better: George Washington was once a baby with parents. Abraham Lincoln was once a baby with parents.

Remember this: When God wanted to change the world, he did it by sending a baby.

Believe it or not, you parents are having more impact on the future than all the presidents and generals and scientists who ever lived. That's because whatever children hear or experience or feel during the early impressionable time in their lives goes into their mental "computers." And those things help determine what kind of an adults they will be.

One man can vividly remember the exact moment and the exact person who crushed his sense of self-worth almost out of existence: His third-grade teacher said, "You are so dumb! Why don't you just drop out and go watch Popeye on TV!" He said, "That remark killed all my incentive to learn." It was years later, after he had served as a medical corpsman in Vietnam, that he finally began to realize he was nowhere near "dumb." He came home, enrolled in college, and later became dean of students at a Seattle college. He is now considered a gifted man, but one thoughtless remark nearly destroyed him.

Call a child stupid, brat, monster or tell him over and over that he does "the dumbest things," and he will live down to precisely the level you set. Sometimes we think because we joke or kid around by using nicknames like runt, ding a ling, or little punk that children know we're teasing. But often they don't. Why take a chance?

One woman said, "I will always remember how my mother attacked me for every little mistake I made. She'd be screaming at me, and the phone would ring; then she would change the tone of her voice and be charming. I always wondered why she treated strangers more politely than she did her own daughter."

Some men and women recall criticisms that were "impossible" to deal with, such as "Why can't you be more like your brother?" One man said he never understood what his mother meant by such remarks. "What was I supposed to do about it? How was I supposed to feel?"

Unfortunately, research indicates that most people's memory banks are crammed with a collection of parental statements seemingly made with the single aim of belittling or rejecting children.

Parenting is difficult, and none of us does a perfect job of training and developing our children. But here are a few principles that will help:

I. Cherish Your Children.
Love them! Nurture them! Bless them! Value them! Spend time with them, and protect them emotionally as well as physically.

II. Challenge Your Children.
Model standards of integrity! Affirm their abilities! Have high expectations, and motivate them toward success.

III. Champion Your Children.
Support them! Defend them! Listen to them, and believe in them!

Many years ago, there was a boy who was considered to be a stupid blockhead. He sat and drew pictures on his slate. He looked around and listened to everybody else. He asked "impossible questions." The kids called him a dunce, and he usually came in at the bottom of his class.

He attended primary school for less than three months. Everyone told him he was dumb.

Finally, he told his mother about hearing the teacher say that he was "addled" and it wouldn't be worthwhile to waste time on him any longer. His mother marched off to school with him and told everybody within range of her voice that her son, Thomas Alva Edison, had more brains than all the teachers and administrators put together.

Edison called his mother the most enthusiastic champion a boy ever had. And from that day forward, he was a changed boy. He said, "She cast over me an influence which has lasted all my life."

A single incident prompted him to turn his negatives into positives. He became a famous inventor that changed the world.

Mothers, you are important. Your example and teaching shape future generations. If you cherish your children, challenge your children, and champion your children, you can change the course of world history! That's why we're honoring you today!

Parenting 101
Psalm 127:3

Today, we're enrolling in Parenting 101. Since all academic courses are composed of a beginning, a middle, and an end, let's look at those three stages of parenting:

I. The Beginning Stage

A mother of three said, "One day, a friend of mine mentioned that she and her husband were thinking of starting a family. She asked, 'What do you think? Should I have a baby?'"

"It will change your life," I told her.

"I know," she said. "No more sleeping in on weekends."

But that's not what I meant at all.

I tried to decide what to tell her. I considered warning her that she will never again read about a tragedy in the newspaper without asking, "What if that had been my child?" That every plane crash, every house fire will haunt her. That when she sees pictures of starving children, she will wonder if anything could be worse than watching your child die.

I looked at her carefully manicured nails and stylish suit and thought that no matter how sophisticated she was, becoming a mother will reduce her to the primitive level of a mama bear protecting her cubs. I wanted my friend to know that everyday decisions would no longer be routine.

My friend's relationship with her husband will also change, but not in the way she thinks. I wish she could understand how much more you can love a man who is careful to powder the baby. I wish my friend could sense the bond she will feel with women throughout history who have tried to stop war and drunk driving.

I hope she will understand why I can think rationally about most issues but become temporarily insane when I discuss the threat of terrorism to my children's future. I want to describe to my friend the joy of seeing your child learn to ride a bike. I want to capture for her the delight of a baby touching the soft fur of a kitten for the first time.

My friend's puzzled look made me realize I had tears in my eyes. "You'll never regret it," I finally said. Then I offered a silent prayer for her and for me and for all of us mere mortal women who enjoy the blessed gift of God—that of being a mother. The psalmist said, "[Children] are indeed a heritage from the LORD" (Ps 127:3).

II. The Middle Stage

Those years are oh so long and yet all too short. During those years you become a real mom. One writer said, "Real moms consider McDonald's 'a basic food group.' A real mom drives her kids to school in her pajamas; a real mom uses her shirt sleeves as a napkin; and a real mom is an imperfect individual just like you and me."

Mothers get a lot of advice and criticism, but it's time to shatter the myth that there's just one right way to mother. First, no one knows the right way. There isn't one. There's only the way that works for you.

Good moms protect their children from the bad stuff in life, but that's tricky. Every mother wants to keep her child from hurting. So when your daughter forgets her homework, it's tempting to just run it up to the school. It's only a few blocks, and then the child won't get points off and her good grades make us all feel good.

When your son strikes out at bat, it's tempting to tell him it's not his fault. It was the dumb pitcher or the blind umpire who was to blame.

When we swallow the myth that good moms protect their kids from all the bad stuff, we often end up overprotecting them. We intercede before they learn from their mistake.

You can try to protect a child from germs by keeping him home from school and church and rejecting his request for playmates, but then again you can't really protect your child from germs. As our children grow, we can only protect them by preparing them for real life. We can teach them how to handle the bad stuff when it comes so they can recognize it and overcome it.

Real moms allow their children to realize that they're not good at everything, that sometimes they will strike out and lose the game and that they might not always make As and Bs. In short, real moms do their children the favor of exposing them to the bad stuff in the world, knowing that learning to cope with the bad stuff will help prepare them for life. That's where the bad stuff happens.

When your child is a baby, you carry her about. It's easier for both of you. She likes it, and you get where you need to go. But as she ages, you have to put your child down and let her learn to walk, to run, to look both ways and cross streets alone, to drive, to date, and to explore. She can't do that if you continue to carry her. Paul describes this growth process: "When I was a child, I spoke like a child, I thought like a child, I reasoned like a child; when I became an adult, I put an end to childish ways" (1 Cor 13:11).

III. The End Stage

We face an empty nest and wonder if we've done our job right. An agriculturalist once asked some farmers, "What ensures a good crop?"

One old fellow said, "Good soil, right seed, proper cultivation."

"But what causes growth?" the researcher persisted.

"I don't know," another farmer said. "It just happens. It's a mystery, I guess. We do what we know how to do, but you never can tell when a drought's going to come along and ruin us, or when we'll have more rain than we know what to do with. Ultimately, it's beyond our control."

It's the same with parenting. We have to admit there is no guarantee that children will turn out the way we want them to. They're human beings who will make their own choices, and there will be surprises. They'll disappoint us in some ways, and they'll also surprise us by accomplishing things we never would have thought possible.

Fortunately, Solomon gave parents a comforting promise: "Train children in the right way, and when old, they will not stray" (Prov 22:6).

Whether your parenting is in the beginning, the middle, or the end stage, remember you are doing God's work here on earth. There's no greater calling than that of guiding, teaching, and loving the next generation. Our future depends on it!

How to Correct Your Kids

Ephesians 6:1-4

Once, a family lost everything in a tragic fire. When somebody expressed sympathy, saying, "I'm sorry, you lost your home," their little girl replied, "Oh no! We still have our home; we just don't have a house to put it in." She was right! Homes are not physical things that can be destroyed by fires. Homes are spiritual units, dependent upon loving relationships.

Edgar A. Guest put it this way in his poem "Home": "It takes a heap o' livin' in a house t' make it home."

You see, homes don't just happen. Homes require firm moral foundations. Our future, our democracy, and our civilization itself depend upon the foundation provided in the home. Our children are our greatest responsibility. The psalmist said, "[Children] are indeed a heritage from the LORD, the fruit of the womb a reward" (Ps 127:3).

In general, parents make two types of mistakes in rearing children. They either become dictators and impose their wills on boys and girls with an absolute authoritarian system, or else they let the boys and girls do whatever they please with a totally permissive system. Neither is effective.

Children must be taught and disciplined but not abused. You can't force another human being to feel and think in a certain way. Harsh punishment causes resentment and rebellion. But neglect is also a form of child abuse.

So how can you correct your kids?

I. Let Them Have Their Way on Nonessentials.

Paul said, "Fathers, do not provoke your children, or they may lose heart" (Col 3:21).

Arbitrary rules and harsh restrictions are counterproductive. Saying "Do it because I said so!" or "You'll do it or else!" makes you a tyrant, not a parent. Even very young children can make choices on many, many issues. We learn to make wise decisions by being allowed to make decisions. If parents dictate every move, children can't grow. Instead of control and domination, children need freedom within limits. Most young people go through a time of testing the boundaries. These limits are necessary, but they should be extended as far as possible, as fast as possible. In other words, as the child shows more maturity and responsibility, then more freedom should be given. There's just so much a parent can do and just so far he can go. After that, it's up to the individual.

Eventually, each child will be on his own, so you must let them make choices about insignificant matters and live with the consequences. You must let them have their way on as many nonessentials as possible.

II. Let Them Have Their Say on Essentials.

Paul said, "Do not provoke your children to anger, but bring them up in the discipline and instruction of the Lord" (Eph 6:4).

Some things are so immoral or damaging or dangerous that parents have to stand firm and hang tough, but even if you must give an ultimatum, the child should still be allowed to state his point of view. Expressing our feelings is a basic human right, and children are no exception. Too often we don't take time to hear our children's concerns and opinions. One woman talks about a thunderstorm that had cut off their electricity. As a matter of last resort, she and her twelve-year-old son actually talked. "History was made," the mother said later, referring to the fact that before this incident, her longest sustained conversation with her child had been perhaps two minutes. "That night, I couldn't do the laundry. I couldn't cook. I couldn't work on the computer. My son couldn't watch TV, play video games, or call his friends, so we talked for hours. I learned about the girls he liked and heard all the latest jokes from school. I discovered his likes and his dislikes and his hopes and his fears. It was an invaluable experience."

It shouldn't take a thunderstorm to force families to communicate with each other. Children who are encouraged to talk about their grievances and angers are much less likely to act them out. So you must maintain a firm stand on the critical issues in their lives, but you must let them have their say—even though you can't let them have their way—on those essential things you disagree about.

III. Be Reasonable and Consistent.

Solomon said, "Train children in the right way, and when old, they will not stray" (Prov 22:6).

Never use ridicule or shame or guilt to manipulate children. Criticize his undesirable behavior if necessary, but not his character.

Also, be flexible and understanding. Realize that there may be reasons for misbehavior. In a large family, the youngest child was withdrawn and paid little attention to his parents. They hoped he would grow out of it. But when he didn't, they began to lose patience with him, and he responded with hostility.

Then a visitor who worked with children noticed something. When his mother scolded him for disobeying, the friend said, "Are you sure he can hear you?" No one had ever considered the possibility that the child might have a physical problem.

An ear specialist found an obstruction that interfered with his hearing. Simple surgery removed it, and he became cooperative and affectionate. You see, there's always a cause for misbehavior. As parents we must find it. Sometimes a child is uncooperative because he's sick or frightened or insecure. Sometimes he needs attention. Sometimes he has a specific learning disability. Until we know why he's acting inappropriately, we can't correct it.

Even when correction is needed, it's wise to let natural consequences provide the punishment as far as possible. If he wastes his allowance, don't give him more. If he gets up too late to eat breakfast, let him do without. If he disobeys at the movies, take him home. Having to suffer a little now may keep him from having to suffer a lot later.

A disciplined child is a happy child, so you must be reasonable and consistent. Being strict one day and lenient the next undermines your credibility. Jesus loved children. He gave all of us a strong warning concerning them. He said, "Let the little children come to me, and do not stop them; for it is to such as these that the kingdom of heaven belongs" (Matt 19:14).

The Canaanites sacrificed their children to their god, Molech. Today we might think child sacrifice is a thing of the past, but we would be wrong. Countless innocent children are being sacrificed on the altar of abuse and neglect. In Detroit, a mother sold her thirteen-year-old daughter to a drug dealer. In Washington, DC, a drunken mother murdered two of her children and tried to kill a third one. In Philadelphia, a six-month-old child died of a drug overdose from cocaine that had been put in her formula. Hundreds of others suffer from passive abuse.

We sacrifice our children to our job, to our convenience, to our pleasure. We sacrifice them to materialism, popularity, and public opinion.

Do you want to correct your kids? Remember, the psalmist said, "Children are indeed a heritage from the LORD" (Ps 127:3).

Your first step is to let your children have their way on nonessentials. Right now, think about your attitudes and habits. Are you a controller? Do you tend to impose your will on others? Can you let your loved ones make their own decisions on issues that aren't immoral or life-threatening? Can you live and let live? Can you tolerate diversity? Resolve to let go and allow as much freedom as possible.

Your next step is to let them have their say on essentials. Right now, think about those important matters that can't be compromised. Can you let your loved ones express their viewpoint? Can you love them even if they disagree with you? Can you listen respectfully and objectively? Can you require compliance without sounding like a dictator? Resolve to hear other opinions without angry, defensive reactions.

Your final step is to be reasonable and consistent. Right now, think about the rules and regulations in your household. Are they rational? Are they based upon true values or merely on habit and public opinions? Resolve to focus on a few significant moral issues instead of a lot of insignificant details.

These are the ways to correct your kids!

Father's Day

I Do! I Really Do!
Ten Essentials for a Happy Marriage

Spiritual love has little to do with emotions. When the Bible says that God loves us, it doesn't just mean he feels a certain way. It means he acts toward us with grace. When the Bible says Christ loves the church, it doesn't just mean he feels a particular emotion. It means he acts toward his people with compassion.

Likewise, when God commands husbands and wives to love each other, he is not commanding us to just feel a particular emotion, but rather to act toward each other with respect and faithfulness. The Apostle Paul said, "Each of you, however, should love his wife as himself, and a wife should respect her husband" (Eph 5:33).

Being "in love," which is infatuation, is not the same as mature love. So let's consider the ten rules for a covenant marriage.

I. There Must Be Commitment.

This includes loyalty and responsibility. We don't promise to be faithful until we get bored or upset. Instead, we promise that our love will be unconditional and permanent. In fact, any marriage over two weeks old can find grounds for divorce if we only look for faults. Instead, we must find reasons to remain committed by looking for the good.

Commitment is a decision and a promise.

II. There Must Be Compatibility.

All of us bring certain expectations to marriage. One wife said, "I thought we got married to be together, but he works all the time." Her husband said, "I thought we'd have a nice home, but there's dirty laundry everywhere." Like most couples, these two entered marriage with very different expectations. This causes trouble.

Compatibility requires agreement on basic values.

III. There Must Be Complementarity.

Most of us are attracted to those who have some opposite traits. We do this to balance the relationship, but later the difference aggravates us. A wife says, "I liked him because he was easygoing, but now he's driving me crazy with his lack of initiative." A husband says, "I liked her because she was confident and reliable, but now I resent her controlling ways."

Why are people attracted to spouses they later resent? Well, we tend to marry someone who is strong where we are weak. That's good, but it can cause conflicts.

Complementarity means that our abilities can differ, but we must appreciate the differences.

IV. There Must Be Communication.

This includes listening and leveling. People feel loved in five ways: words, gifts, physical touch, time together, and acts of service.

Most husbands and wives speak different love languages. The words may be familiar, but the meaning is misunderstood.

For instance, after their golden anniversary celebration, one husband said, "You're tired, dear. Would you like some toast and tea?" "Oh, yes!" she replied. However, when he brought it, she exploded: "It looks like on our special day, you could give me the best part?" "But I did," he protested.

You see, for fifty years he'd been giving her the heel of the bread—which to him was the best part—and for fifty years she'd been feeling that he had been giving her the scraps.

Communication is expressing our feelings clearly and making sure we're understood.

V. There Must Be Competence.

This includes knowledge and skills. We must use a little common sense in dealing with disagreements.

Don't build up resentments and then explode.

Don't blame, accuse, insult, or call names.

Don't bring up every past grievance and dump them all at once.

But do express your needs and complaints in "I" language. Say "I get upset," not "You upset me."

Do face the problem together. That way, it's not me against you; instead, it's us against this unproductive situation.

And do be realistic. An old lady overheard a young wife say, "My relationship is pretty good, but it's not perfect." The veteran wife interrupted, "Listen, my dear, when it comes to marriage, pretty good is perfect.

Competence enables couples to achieve win/win solutions.

VI. There Must Be Companionship.

Our mate should be our best friend. All of us have physical, emotional, and intellectual needs. If most of these needs are met, we feel cared for. But if most of these needs aren't met, we feel neglected.

When couples have very different needs, it's difficult to sustain the marriage. If one person needs intimacy and the other needs independence, there are problems. If one person is oriented to spiritual values and the other is materialistic, there are problems.

Companionship requires a sharing of leisure time activities.

VII. There Must Be Cooperation.

This includes give and take, negotiation and compromise. Selfishness must be overcome for the sake of the union. You must form a team.

A man watching Olympic-class boat crews race on a lake asked the winners, "What is the single most important thing in crew racing?"

"Teamwork," they replied, almost in unison and without hesitation. "Everyone must pull together."

It's the same in marriage. Cooperation involves concern and mutual goals.

VIII. There Must Be Compassion.

This includes understanding and patience. An older couple said, "We had a terrible time when we were first married. We almost separated. Then we made a list of all the good things about each other. This was hard because we had become so hostile. But we kept at it, and when we finished, we framed that list and hung it on the wall above our bed."

The husband continued, "If we have a secret, this is it: We agreed to read these things at least once a day until we got our problems straightened out. The more I considered the good she saw in me, the more I tried to be like that; the more she considered the good I saw in her, the more she tried to be like that. This practice saved our marriage.

Compassion sees the good and overlooks the bad.

IX. There Must Be Courtesy.

This includes kindness, politeness, and respect. Too often we are nicer to neighbors and even strangers than we are to our loved ones.

Once, a young lady was questioned about her choice of a husband. She said, "When I was with Bill, I thought he was the most wonderful person in the world." Her friend asked, "Then why didn't you marry Bill instead of Jim?"

"Because," she replied, "when I'm with Jim, I feel like I'm the most wonderful person in the world."

Courtesy on our part makes our mates feel good about themselves.

X. There Must Be Caution.

This includes vigilance and thoughtfulness. Temptations are everywhere. Don't put your relationship at risk. Don't take your marriage for granted.

It's helpful to regularly spend five minutes with each other in meditation:

In the first minute: Recall the qualities that made you fall in love in the first place.

In the second minute: Think about life without your mate. Sometimes we don't appreciate things until they're gone.

In the third minute: Consider all the people who would be hurt if your marriage failed.

In the fourth minute: Read the Apostle Paul's definition of love: "Love is patient; love is kind; love is not envious or boastful or arrogant or rude. It does not insist on its own way; it is not irritable or resentful; it does not rejoice in wrongdoing, but rejoices in the truth. It bears all things, believes all things, hopes all things, endures all things. Love never ends" (1 Cor 13:4–8).

In the fifth minute: Pray and admit your part in any problems. Express gratitude for the blessings. Promise to respect your mate and honor your marriage covenant.

If you will do this sincerely, your relationship will remain strong and love will prevail.

Children Are Different

Proverbs 22:6

Solomon says, "Train up a child in the way he should go: and when he is old, he will not depart from it" (Prov 22:6, KJV). This means each child has his own special personality. No two are alike. You can't treat your children the same way. You can't discipline your children the same way. You can't expect your children to respond in the same way.

Every child is unique, but they do tend to fall into four general types. Of course, none is exact, and they often have traits of two or more types.

Some children are born with social abilities. They get along with everyone. They love adventure and excitement. They are good at telling stories and playing games. They love parties and have many friends. They are popular and full of life.

But, like all of us, they have some weak areas: They may try to do too many things and join too many clubs. They may be forgetful. They may not finish every task. They may get bored easily and shirk their duties in order to have fun. They may exaggerate and tell tall tales.

As to discipline, these little entertainers need to be kept very busy. They need to have opportunities to perform. They need many social activities. They need training in honesty and responsibility. They need to develop the ability to focus on important things.

Their motto should be "Do your work first; get it done. Then you can play and have more fun!"

Other children are born with organizational skills. They are strong-willed. They have definite desires and opinions. They are usually hard workers with a lot of determination. They do well in achieving success and completing projects. These children like to be in control, and they can be surprisingly responsible and practical.

However, their weak areas include bossiness and impatience. They tend to throw temper tantrums.

As to discipline, these little controllers need to be given as much self-control as possible. They need to be allowed to make as many personal decisions as possible. They need to have choices and challenges, but they must also learn to share and cooperate and adapt to other people's needs and actions.

A few children are born with deep sensitivity and adult-type tendencies. They may seem to be four going on forty at times. They have strengths in areas of duty and responsibility. They may be perfectionists, and they care deeply about having things "just right." They are often loners and don't seem to need a lot of social interaction.

They have empathy for others and may cry about seeing starving children on TV. Sometimes they have artistic or scientific interests.

As to discipline, these little philosophers actually need very little outside discipline because they are hard on themselves and try to measure up to such high standards. They require special consideration and careful understanding. They are easily hurt and can be fragile and vulnerable. They need to be encouraged to relax and accept life in an imperfect world.

Some children are easygoing peacemakers. They are very cooperative and adaptable. Everybody likes them. Sometimes these little ones are neglected or ignored because they don't demand attention like the entertainers. They don't try to take over every situation like the controllers. They aren't as sensitive and perfectionistic as the philosophers.

As to discipline, they do need respect and guidance. Sometimes they need to be pushed to accomplish tasks and be more responsible. They are not usually competitive or opinionated. Even though they avoid conflict and hesitate to confront others, they can be stubborn and often resort to covert means of opposition. Instead of starting fights or openly disagreeing, they use passive-aggressive methods of getting their needs met.

So children are all different, but they are all valuable and special to Jesus. He said, "Unless you change and become like children, you will never enter the kingdom of heaven. Whoever becomes humble like this child is the greatest in the kingdom of heaven. Whoever welcomes one such child in my name welcomes me. "If any of you put a stumbling block before one of these little ones who believe in me, it would be better for you if a great millstone were fastened around your neck and you were drowned in the depth of the sea" (Matt 18:3–6).

He also said, "Let the little children come to me, and do not stop them; for it is to such as these that the kingdom of heaven belongs" (Matt 19:14).

Our children are our greatest assets, but they are also our greatest responsibility, so don't ever try to make Susie be like Sarah or Freddie be like Joe. Each one is unique with special strengths and weaknesses. Each one has a right to have their deepest needs met and their greatest desires fulfilled.

How to Bless Your Family

(An Acrostic)
Luke 11:9-13

What are you doing today that will still be important 100 years from now? What are you doing today that will influence future lives for good or for evil? What are you doing today that will change the world in a significant way?

Well, if you have children, then your relationship with them and your impact on them will be your most important legacy.

The family is the smallest unit of society. It should be the one place where you are accepted, loved, and valued—the one place where you can be open and honest. God established the family: "Then the Lord God said, 'It is not good that the man should be alone; I will make him a helper as his partner.' Therefore a man leaves his father and his mother and clings to his wife, and they become one flesh" (Gen 2:18, 24).

Marriages are part of God's plan. Solomon said, "He who finds a wife finds a good thing, and obtains favor from the Lord." (Prov 18:22a).

There are many benefits of a family. The writer of Ecclesiastes said, "Two are better than one, because they have a good reward for their toil. For if they fall, one will lift up the other; but woe to one who is alone and falls and does not have another to help" (Eccl 4:9-10).

Our world, our nation, and our communities are in trouble in the twenty-first century because our families are disintegrating. One teen expressed it this way: "I know my name, but I don't know who I am. I am here, but I don't know where I am. I know where I came from, but I don't know where I'm going. I'm supposed to be living the 'happiest days of my life,' and I'm crying."

Divorce is common. Domestic abuse is rampant.

What can we do about these problems? Well, God gave a promise to Abraham that still applies to us: "I will make of you a great nation, and I will bless you, and make your name great, so that you will be a blessing" (Gen 12:2).

How can we bless our families and enable them to bless others?

B Reminds Us We Can Believe in Them.

This means to see their value and give them confidence. Children are to be cherished. Jesus gave them a top priority. He believed in little boys and girls. He said, "'Let the little children come to me; do not stop them; for it is to such as these that the kingdom of God belongs.' And he took them up in his arms, laid his hands on them, and blessed them" (Mark 10:14, 16).

A few years ago, actor Kirk Douglas wrote his autobiography. He recalls that his mother was warm and supportive, but he remembers his father as stern, strict, cold, unaccustomed to giving words of encouragement or a pat on the back. However, after attending a school performance in which Douglas sang, Douglas's father rewarded him with ice cream. Though he didn't have much to say about the performance, Douglas cherished that moment of connection.

In order to bless your family, build their self-esteem, give them approval, and let them know you believe in them.

L Reminds Us That We Can Love Them.

This means showing affection and concern. We can do this through both words and deeds. Solomon said, "From the fruit of the mouth one's stomach is satisfied; the yield of the lips brings satisfaction. Death and life are in the power of the tongue, and those who love it will eat its fruits" (Prov 18:20–21a).

Love between husbands and wives sets the stage for sons and daughters. Paul said, "The husband should give to his wife her conjugal rights, and likewise the wife to her husband" (1 Cor 7:3).

Unconditional love is a parent's best gift. In order to bless your family, say "I love you," and give a lot of hugs.

E Reminds Us That We Can Enjoy Them.

The writer of Ecclesiastes said, "Enjoy life with the wife whom you love, all the days of your vain life that are given you under the sun" (Eccl 9:9).

This means family life must include more than work and worry. Jesus said, "Therefore I tell you, do not worry about your life, what you will eat or what you will drink, or about your body, what you will wear. Is not life more than food, and the body more than clothing?" (Matt 6:25).

There must be some rest and recreation. A little fun is necessary.

Once, an old woman recalled a memory from her childhood. She tells of her busy family on the farm, taking a moment to fly kites. It was perfect kite flying weather, and the whole family joined in. Years later the girl had her own family and her mother was visiting. The woman's child asked to go to the park, but the woman was busy. Her mother remarked on how the day reminded her of the day they flew kites many years ago.

So they went to the park!

Another decade later the woman's brother was recalling his memories as a POW, and spoke of how he thought of the kite flying when he was a prisoner.

Years later, the woman's father died. Her mother reminisced about how much fun they had on that kite flying day.

In families, it's often the little things that matter most. In order to bless your family, make some wonderful memories and enjoy them.

S Reminds Us That We Can Support Them.

This means giving encouragement. It means providing the necessary resources. Paul said, "Anyone who does not provide for their relatives, and especially for their own household, has denied the faith and is worse than an unbeliever" (1 Tim 5:8).

Jesus expects us to give good things to our mates and our children. He said, "If your child asks for a fish, will give a snake instead of a fish? Or if the child asks for an egg, will give a scorpion?" (Luke 11:11–12).

A poet wrote:

> Give them food. Give them clothes.
> These are needful—heaven knows.
> Give them bikes and cowboy boots;
> But first of all, give them roots.

In order to bless your family, fill their needs physically, emotionally, and spiritually. Support them.

S Reminds Us That We Can Shape Them.

This means being an example and a teacher. Solomon said, "The righteous walk in integrity—happy are the children who follow them" (Prov 20:7).

"Train children in the right way, and when old, they will not stray" (Prov 22:6).

This training should be positive, not negative. Too many parents train up their children in the way they should not go instead of training them in the way they should go. They emphasize what's wrong instead of what's right. A lot of rules and taboos can cause resentment and rebellion. Paul knew this. He said, "Fathers, do not provoke your children to anger" (Eph 6:4).

"Fathers, do not provoke your children, or they may lose heart" (Col 3:21).

Instead, show proper behavior and emphasize right responses. In order to bless your family, be an example. Pass on moral principles and shape their character.

Remember, all the money in the world can't buy a home. It can only buy a house to put it in. A real home must be built with love and blessed by the Lord. An Old Testament scripture says, "You shall put these words of mine in your heart and soul, and you shall bind them as a sign on your hand, and fix them as an emblem on your forehead. Teach them to your children, talking about them when you are at home and when you are away, when you lie down and when you rise. Write them on the doorposts of your house and on your gates" (Deut 11:18a–20).

Many homes in Switzerland obey this command literally. Verses are painted or carved over the doorways of older houses.

Think about this: If we put mottos on our homes in America, what message would your home give to a watching world? How many of us today are willing to say with Joshua, "As for me and my household, we will serve the LORD" (Josh 24:15b)?

Let's bless our families by believing, loving, enjoying, supporting, and shaping each other to the glory of God. Forest Witcraft said, "A hundred years from now it will not matter what my bank account was, the sort of house I lived in, or the kind of car I drove... but the world may be different because I was important in the life of a child."

Bless your family today. It's your most important task and the only one that will still be important centuries from now.

How to Challenge Your Children
Proverbs 4:1-10

A naturalist watched as an eagle taught its young to fly. She took the eaglet on her broad back and carried him high into the air. At the proper moment she tilted her wings and slid him off into space. Fluttering and screeching, the little bird drifted down. As he fell, his parent circled around him. Then, before the eaglet crashed on the rocks below, she glided underneath and caught him on her strong wings. This action was repeated many times.

Now, this process looked risky and even cruel, but in order for the eaglet to become independent, it was necessary, Likewise, children must mature and become responsible. The writer of Ecclesiastes said, "Remember your Creator in the days of your youth, before the evil days come."

Neglected children are crippled, but overprotected children are also crippled. Challenges strengthen us. New Zealand has few dangerous animals or reptiles. It is also the home of more flightless birds than any other country in the world. Scientists believe there is a connection between these two facts. Since there were no predators to fear, the birds didn't need to spread their wings and fly. With no necessity to fly, they soon lost their ability to fly. It's the same in human life.

One parent spent an hour every morning getting her fourteen-year-old daughter ready for school. She would call, beg, and threaten to get her up and then later write excuse notes explaining away her lateness. Finally, she bought an alarm clock and told the teenager that from now on she must take the responsibility for herself. At first the teen griped and whined. She would forget to set the alarm or wouldn't hear it. But when she overslept and had to face the principal without an excuse, she had to take the consequences. After a few days of that, she got up, got ready, and got to school on time.

In order to learn, some hardships are necessary. So how can you challenge your children?

I. Help Them Develop Self-Esteem.

Jesus said, "Do not be afraid; you are of more value than many sparrows" (Matt 10:31). People need to have a sense of their basic worth as persons! They need to feel that they deserve their space on earth. We must not kill a child's spirit or destroy a child's self-worth.

Now, parents can't actually give self-worth, but they can help a child develop it. In order to do that, let children see positive, warm feelings on your face. Listen carefully when they express feelings and opinions. Find activities you can do together. Use frequent and sincere praise.

Don't ridicule or shame children. Share your own problems and joys with your children. Set an example of honesty and concern. Teach them strong moral values, and let them accept responsibilities for their own actions. Show them alternatives to undesirable behavior. Point out how mistakes might be prevented by thinking ahead.

These things will help them develop self-esteem.

II. Help Them Develop Self-Confidence.

Paul said, "I can do all things through him who strengthens me" (Phil 4:13).

Insecure people are unproductive and often destructive. Some who lack confidence withdraw and do nothing. They are like the man who was given one talent and immediately hid it in the ground. Jesus said, "But the one who had received the one talent went off and dug a hole in the ground and hid his master's money" (Matt 25:18).

Others who lack confidence react in an opposite direction. They become overly aggressive and try to cover their inadequacies by becoming braggarts and bullies.

Children need security and assurance and support. Most people can remember being terrified when they were left with a babysitter, or had to speak in front of the class, or were caught out in a thunderstorm. Yet those same people often dismiss similar fears in their own children. Instead, we must recognize anxieties and insecurities. There are four major fears among children. The greatest is the fear of abandonment and rejection. The child may refuse to go to bed, fearful of being left out. Or a child caught up in a divorce may feel abandoned by the parent who is no longer in the home. They may worry that the remaining parent will also leave him.

Then there is the fear of failure. Here, the child may misbehave as a distraction. Facing consequences of the misbehavior is less frightening than facing tasks that may bring failure.

There is also the fear of humiliation. Even seemingly trivial things, such as not wearing the right clothes or having the right hairstyle, fall into this category. These things aren't trivial to an insecure teenager.

Finally, there is the fear of objects, people, and situations. Preschoolers vividly imagine there are monsters in their closets and under their beds. Unfamiliar events are frightening when a child doesn't know what to expect, such as the first day at a new childcare center.

Lying, stealing, and hyperactivity are signs of fear in some children. Parents should acknowledge the fears and then provide ways for children to work through them. Let the child express himself, and never ridicule or make light of a child's fears.

These actions will help them develop self-confidence.

III. Help Them Develop Self-Discipline.

Solomon said, "Listen to advice and accept instruction, that you may gain wisdom for the future" (Prov 19:20).

A disciplined person is a happy and successful person. Just obeying is not enough, because authority figures won't always be available. Instead, we must develop self-discipline. Researchers have found that students with better grades and achievement test scores had parents who encouraged both independence and discipline. These parents allowed their children to make choices and participate in decisions.

In fact, most young people want discipline. When sociologists interviewed teenagers on what they wanted from their parents, this is what they said:

1. Trust us! We want our parents to expect the best of us, not fear the worst.

2. Include us! We want parents who will stand beside us, not over us. We appreciate guidance in important matters, but after we've proven ourselves to have mature judgment, we don't want to be nagged about every little thing.

3. Give us responsibility! We want our share of family tasks, but we'd like to know who's to do what and why.

High expectations stimulate growth in children, so you must help them develop self-discipline.

Solomon said, "The father of the righteous will greatly rejoice; he who begets a wise son will be glad in him" (Prov 23:24).

Paul said, "And whoever does not provide for relatives, and especially for family members, has denied the faith and is worse than an unbeliever" (1 Tim 5:8).

We provide for our family by setting limits and requiring responsibility. We desperately need our next generation to be people who are responsible! In order to have that, we must challenge our children!

Your first step is to help them develop self-esteem. Right now, think about your children and loved ones. Do you show them that they are important? Do you refrain from unkind names and reprimands? Do you treat them at least as courteously as you do your neighbors?

Your next step is to help them develop self-confidence. Right now, think about your children and loved ones. Do you take their insecurities and fears seriously? Do you help them express and deal with their anxieties in a productive way? Do you allow them to attempt tasks and encourage them to follow through? Do you emphasize their strengths and successes?

Your final step is to help them develop self-discipline. Right now, think about your children and loved ones. Do you insist on appropriate behavior? Do you follow through on consequences? Do you provide a mature example in moral matters?

Parents, your most important task and responsibility is to protect, support, and challenge your children so they can become mature, productive adults.

What Is Love to a Child?

Love means different things to different people. It can be romance or friendship or concern and protection. But love is an abstract term that children don't understand. Love is something that must be experienced. Perhaps one reason boys get into more trouble than girls is because parents are more prone to express their love for their daughters. They tend to think their sons don't need this interaction. Well, they're wrong. Sons need love every bit as much as daughters, and maybe even more.

So what is love to a child?

I. Love Is Touch.

At first a baby learns through touch. It is held and stroked and hugged. In fact, babies who do not receive the loving touch die.

During World War II, as Paris was being bombed by Nazi planes, a French doctor made a remarkable discovery. He was appalled by the high death rate among babies in shelters and orphanages. Upon closer examination he discovered that babies who received regular affection fared better than the others. Intrigued, he conducted a brief experiment, dividing the babies into two groups. Both groups of infants were cared for physically. They were fed identical diets and had their diapers changed at regular intervals. The only difference between the two groups was that one group of babies received hugs and kisses from their caretakers. They were cradled and held and rocked and patted. The other group received no affection from their caretakers but were cared for and provided for in every other way.

The babies who were cuddled and loved not only grew but thrived. The other babies, who had all their needs met except their need for love and affection, did not grow as fast. They cried more and succumbed to more illnesses.

These two groups of babies were different only in the amount of love and affection they received, but what a difference that made in their health and development. The study revealed that children who are not treated with affection do not develop properly.

The physical blessing of children is one of the traditions strict Jewish families observe. At the beginning of each Sabbath, the father kisses each child's forehead and pronounces a blessing.

When it comes to touch, Jesus sets the example. The scriptures say, "Little children were being brought to him in order that he might lay his hands on them and pray. The disciples spoke sternly to those who brought them; but Jesus said, 'Let the little children come to me, and do not stop them; for it is to such as these that the kingdom of heaven belongs.' And he laid his hands on them and went on his way" (Matt 19:13–15).

II. Love Is Talk.

As soon as possible, a child begins to hear and express feelings in words. How we speak is as important as what we speak.

Children need a lot of encouragement. We need to give about ten compliments and positive statements for every one complaint or negative statement. Words can hurt, and words can heal. Jesus certainly validated and elevated children. The scriptures say, "Unless you change and become like children, you will never enter the kingdom of heaven. Whoever becomes humble like this child is the greatest in the kingdom of heaven. Whoever welcomes one such child in my name welcomes me. "If any of you put a stumbling block before one of these little ones who believe in me, it would be better for you if a great millstone were fastened around your neck and you were drowned in the depth of the sea" (Matt 18:3–6).

Don't you imagine that little child was positively influenced by this incident?

III. Love Is Time.

We speak of quality time, not quantity of time, but some amount of quantity is required. Research has found that the average parent only spends a few minutes each day with each child.

After returning home from yet another stress-filled, pressure-packed, intensely busy, and highly aggravating day, a young businessman slumped into his easy chair to read the paper and to try to relax. His curious little eight-year-old son approached and asked, "Daddy, how much do you get paid per hour?"

Irritated and annoyed by the question, the father snapped, "I don't know, twenty dollars or so, I guess. Why are you asking me questions like that? Can't you see I'm tired?

"I'm sorry, Daddy," the little boy said, and ran out of the room. In a little while, his son was back with another question: "Daddy, can I borrow seven dollars and fifty-five cents?"

This time, the young father really got aggravated, and he snapped, "This is ridiculous! It's nighttime. You don't need money now. Just go to your room! I'm not in the mood for your games tonight!"

Later, the father felt guilty for being so rough on his son, so he went to check on him. "Son, I'm sorry I was so short with you earlier. I guess I had a bad day at the office. Sure, I'll loan you the money. Here it is—seven dollars and fifty-five cents. But tell me, what do you need it for?"

The little boy smiled and reached under his pillow. He pulled out a box, which contained some dollar bills and coins. "Thanks, Dad. This is great! Now I have enough!"

"Enough for what, Son?" his father asked.

"Enough to buy an hour of your time, Dad."

Jesus always took time for children: "Then he took a little child and put it among them; and taking it in his arms, he said to them, 'Whoever welcomes one such child in my name welcomes me, and whoever welcomes me welcomes not me but the one who sent me.'" (Mark 9:36–37).

Fathers, your children are your most significant legacy. Don't blow it.

Theodore Roosevelt once stopped short a cabinet meeting to keep a date he had to play with his sons, saying, "I learned many years ago that you can never keep children waiting."

Almost all fathers say they love their children—and almost all fathers do love their children—but many don't know how to show it. Your children can't read your mind. Your children must draw conclusions based on your behavior. So touch your children with a pat on the back, an arm around the shoulder, and a sincere hug.

Talk with your children. Use encouraging words and wise teachings.

Spend time with your children. Nothing is more important.

Comedian Jeff Foxworthy gives an example: Even with one foot in the show-business fast lane, Foxworthy says he has purposely made his life as normal as it can be. "I was invited to host a dinner at the White House once, but I couldn't go because it was the same night as my daughter's play at school," he said. "Twenty years from now, the president won't remember if I came to the White House or not, but my daughter will remember if I came to her play."

No matter how busy or famous you are, every child needs touch, talk, and time! Fathers, it's your responsibility to fill these needs.

Graduation

The Gospel According to Humpty Dumpty

1 John 1:9

There's a nursery rhyme that goes like this:
>Humpty Dumpty sat on a wall.
>Humpty Dumpty had a great fall.
>All the king's horses and all the king's men
>Couldn't put Humpty together again.

I. Humpty Dumpty Sat on a Wall.

Let's look at this situation. What's happening here? This was a high wall. It was a narrow wall. Now, why on earth would an egg choose to sit on such a high, narrow wall?

Maybe he wanted to see over on the other side. Maybe the birds made him do it. Maybe he just liked to climb and do scary things.

Surely he didn't think about the consequences. Didn't he realize he was fragile? Didn't he realize eggs break? Didn't he realize the danger of his position?

He didn't seem to. He just sat there on that wall without a care in the world. But Humpty Dumpty took a risk. He made a mistake, and he was about to suffer the consequences.

Now, what should Humpty Dumpty have done? Well, for one thing, he should have stayed off that wall. There were warm nests available. There was soft hay. There was green grass. There was white sand—all safe places to play.

But no. He had to push his limits and perch on a dangerous wall.

Are we like that? Do we do dangerous and foolish things? Do we take unnecessary risks?

Young people, remember Humpty Dumpty and stay away from danger. Don't go to those parties where kids drink and smoke. Don't get into those cars with drivers who speed and take chances. Don't join a group that breaks the law or bends the rules or deceives parents and teachers.

Paul said, "abstain from every form of evil" (1 Thess 5:22).

We don't have to tell you: You know the wrong crowd and the wrong hangouts and the wrong roads. You know who you should associate with, and where you should go, and what you should do.

Humpty Dumpty would never have fallen if he hadn't gotten on that wall. He knew eggshells can shatter, but he probably thought, "That won't happen to me. I'm different. Other eggs may be stupid, but not me! Other eggs may be vulnerable, but not me! Other eggs may be unlucky, but not me!"

Too many of us think we're smarter, so we won't get caught with that cigarette or that beer. We think we're stronger, so we won't get beaten up or shot if we're with a gang. We think we're luckier, so we won't be the one to catch a disease or die from an overdose.

But that's not true! It can happen to anyone! The scripture says, "Be sure your sin will find you out" (Num 32:23).

Unfortunately, in Humpty Dumpty's case, it did.

II. Humpty Dumpty Had a Great Fall.

It seems the most awful, horrible, terrible thing happened. That poor little egg crashed. We don't know why. Maybe he was showing off. Maybe he got overbalanced. Maybe someone pushed him. Maybe the wind blew him off.

Anyway, that doesn't matter. What matters is that Humpty Dumpty fell. Blaming the wind or an overactive rooster won't fix the problem.

As we said, Humpty Dumpty took a risk. He made a mistake, and he suffered the consequences. Sin will take you further than you planned to go! Sin will keep you longer than you planned to stay! Sin will cost you more than you planned to pay!

Paul said, "The wages of sin is death" (Rom 6:23).

Humpty Dumpty didn't plan to smash on the hard ground on the other side of that wall. He didn't plan to lay there in that embarrassing condition all day while horses and men tried to fix him. And he certainly didn't plan to break his shell into a thousand pieces and let his yolk soak into the dirt.

No! He didn't plan on any of these things because, in fact, he didn't plan at all.

That was his problem! Mankind is a Humpty Dumpty, and mankind has had a great fall. The scripture says, "All have sinned and fall short of the glory of God" (Rom 3:23). We've climbed and stretched and reached for more power, more money, more possessions, more weapons, and more pleasure, and we've come crashing down.

Divorce shatters families. Crime shatters communities. War shatters nations. Today's world is fractured, fragmented, splintered, and split apart. That's what happened to Humpty Dumpty. But the worst is yet to come.

III. All the King's Horses and All the King's Men Couldn't Put Humpty Together Again.

This refutes our overly optimistic outlook. We're a "can do" generation. We take pride in our achievements. We can fix anything. Get a disease; there are drugs to cure it. Commit a crime; there are sharp lawyers to beat the rap. Wreck your car; there are insurance adjusters to replace it.

Unfortunately, some things can't be fixed. Once a deed is done, it can't be undone. Horses and people can't make things right.

Life moves forward. Time marches on. When those hurtful words are said or those careless deeds are done, nothing can take them back.

When our reputation is ruined and our relationships are destroyed, all the horsepower of science, all the might of knowledge, all the discoveries and insights and military victories cannot put us together again.

Power and knowledge are good. They are gifts of God. They are "the king's horses," but they cannot fix fallen souls.

All our technological experts and medical personnel, all the attorneys and politicians and academic professors cannot put us together again.

Skill and education are good. They are gifts of God. They are "the king's men," but they cannot fix fallen souls!

Like Humpty Dumpty, our characters and hopes and dreams are fragmented. As long as we are selfish, irresponsible, and uncommitted, our lives will remain shattered.

So what hope do we have? "The king's horses" have failed. "The king's men" have failed. There is only one hope—that is "the King" himself! Let us trust him for help. Let us ask him to put us together again. He created us in the beginning, and he is able and willing to re-create us. The scriptures say, "A new heart I will give you, and a new spirit I will put within you" (Ezek 36:26). "If anyone is in Christ, there is a new creation: everything old has passed away; see, everything has become new!" (2 Cor 5:17).

Even though we've fallen, the image of God is still within us. We want to be whole. Like Humpty Dumpty, we have fallen. Our lives are shattered, but God can make us whole. He specializes in making things whole. When a desperately sick woman came to Christ, he said, "Take heart... your faith has made you well" (Matt 9:22).

When the invalid by the pool obeyed Jesus, the scripture says, "At once the man was made well" (John 5:9).

When the poor lame beggar responded, Peter said, "This man is standing before you in good health by the name of Jesus Christ of Nazareth" (Acts 4:10).

So the moral of the story is this: If you climb a high wall and lose your balance, you'll fall. Once you've fallen, all the things in the world and all the people in the world can't put you together again.

But God can!

Once, an egg went from the farm to the supermarket. He was bought along with eleven others and taken for a ride. Then, as he was being stored in the refrigerator, something happened. He fell and, like Humpty Dumpty, was shattered into a hundred pieces.

Was he doomed? Would he end up in the garbage? No! Fortunately, his owner was not just a cook. He was an artist. He carefully gathered the bits of shell and carried them to his studio.

After days of arrangement and design, the plain old broken egg had been transformed into a wonderful little piece of art.

Of course, that egg will never be the same. Its shell is still cracked. The white has evaporated, and the yolk is gone. But it has a new life as a thing of beauty and wholeness.

Later, as it sat in a museum among priceless Fabergé creations, a viewer murmured, "It was broken to become more beautiful!"

This can happen to you too! Those hurts and pains and cracks don't have to destroy you. If you're broken, God can make you beautiful. Let him rearrange the broken pieces of your life. Let him make you whole again.

Like the egg, you will never be quite the same. The scars will still be there, but you can have a new life. All the king's horses and all the king's men couldn't put you together again.

But God can!

Life Is a Game, and Here Are the Rules

1 Corinthians 9:24; Hebrews 12:1

If a man jumps off the Empire State building and yells, "I defy the law of gravity!," he's going to be unpleasantly surprised. Natural laws can't be broken. And there are natural laws in the human dimension that are just as real and unchangeable as those in the physical dimension. Successful people learn and follow those principles. Unsuccessful people do not learn and do not follow those principles.

So life is a game with definite rules, and we can't change them. If we break the rules, we lose the game. If we obey the rules, we win the game. It's as simple as that. Paul said, "Do you not know that in a race the runners all compete, but only one receives the prize? Run in such a way that you may win it" (1 Cor 9:24).

These truths have universal applications. There are no exceptions. Furthermore, they are not suggestions or recommendations. They are statements of reality.

I. You Are Responsible.

When you have a problem, you must either change the circumstances or change yourself. You can't change anybody else. Too many of us point fingers, pass the buck, and blame others, but this doesn't solve the problem.

II. You Get Out of Life What You Put In.

For most, it takes energy and determination to achieve success. Also, your thoughts and feelings and actions must match. Wishful thinking and positive speaking won't accomplish anything without productive action. Someone said, "If the mind can conceive it and the heart can believe it, then the body can achieve it."

III. You Can't Skip Steps.

It's impossible to take shortcuts in the developmental process. On a ten-point scale, if you're on level five and want to move to level eight, you must first complete steps six and seven. This includes "deferred gratification." This means being willing to work and wait for possessions and pleasures.

It means saving before spending. It means scrubbing floors or waiting tables while studying to be a doctor instead of taking a better-paying job now that has no future possibilities. In short, you must pay first to play later.

IV. You Must Recognize What's Important.

You must set priorities and say "No!" to lesser things. You wouldn't go into a famous art museum and spend your whole time looking at a mop bucket in the corner. You wouldn't escape from a burning home carrying a sack of garbage while leaving priceless treasures behind.

V. Every Mistake Teaches a Lesson.

In fact, the lessons will be repeated until they are learned. The productive approach to a mistake or failure is to acknowledge it, correct it, and learn from it.

We learn through trial and error. Overcoming obstacles makes us stronger.

VI. You Only Win When Everybody Wins.

This may sound contradictory, but it's not. The game of life isn't like a football competition or a chess contest, with one winner and one loser. On a seesaw, when I go up, you go down. Some people put others down, thinking that will allow them to go up. But that's not true in life. Life is like an elevator: Everyone goes up or down together.

Bullies may use their positions or their money to win at any cost, but the loser always comes back to fight another day.

VII. Balance Is Essential.

Anything can be wrong if it's taken to extremes. Opposites can be equally unproductive. One man said, "My old Sunday school teacher emphasized the principle of moderation. She said, 'Movies? Sure, but not too many, and pick the good ones. Baseball? You bet, but don't play so much that you neglect your homework.'"

This may sound terribly old-fashioned, but it teaches us something that is still true today. It teaches us that there is good in almost everything if you control it instead of letting it control you. Furthermore, there is bad in almost everything if you carry it to extremes and become addicted.

Yes, Jesus wanted us to be happy and successful. He said, "I came that they may have life, and have it abundantly" (John 10:10).

And we can only have that abundant life if we follow the rules. Maturity doesn't necessarily come with age. It comes with acceptance of responsibility.

Maturity is when you not only know how to dress yourself, but you also remember to put your dirty clothes in the hamper after you take them off.

Maturity is when you are not only old enough to drive the car, but you also pay for the gas you use.

Yes, life is a game, and you are the player. An advertisement for tennis rackets showed Jimmy Connors making a lot of fancy shots. The narrator said, "If this racket can win at Wimbledon, it can certainly handle your matches."

A man bought one of those rackets and played all summer. But he lost all summer. That's because the racket didn't win at Wimbledon. Jimmy Connors did.

It's the same in the game of life. It's not the things we have, or the places we live, or the people we know that ensures success. You, and you alone, determine whether you win or lose.

Furthermore, you owe it to yourself and to the world to fill your role. If one hundred people stood around the Statue of Liberty, no two of them would see exactly the same thing. Each one's unique viewpoint is determined by his position and angle of observation. None is wrong when he describes what he sees, even though it may be totally different from what another person sees.

Likewise, life gives each person a different view of truth, depending on his background and experience. None is wrong when he describes what he sees, even though it may be entirely different from what others see.

Each has a right, and indeed an obligation, to share his particular view as fully as possible. Be what you are! Be nothing but what you are! But be all that you are!

If you don't live authentically and reflect your view of life, then there will forever be a you-shaped hole in the fabric of the universe. Imagine that the total of human existence is a huge jigsaw puzzle. Each piece is essential. They all interlock and connect into a whole. If a single little odd-shaped, one-of-a-kind fragment is lost or mutilated, the picture will never be complete.

In the game of life, three things are essential:

1. You must prepare. Unfortunately, some of us think we don't need to study and practice. That's not true.

According to legend, a man was riding along one night when a voice out of the darkness said, "Stop! Get down and pick up some pebbles. In the morning you will be both glad and sorry!"

The man was puzzled, but he obeyed. When dawn came, he reached into his bag and was astonished to find that the pebbles were all diamonds.

Then he understood the strange statement. He was indeed both glad and sorry. He was glad that he had picked up some pebbles, but he was also sorry he hadn't picked up more.

Education is like that. You'll always be glad for what you have achieved but sorry you didn't get more. Preparation is essential!

2. You must participate! You need to get off the bench and get into the game. Too many of us sit on the sidelines as spectators. Too many young people don't vote or make their voice heard on crucial issues. But to make a difference, you must get involved. All of us must participate!

3. You must persevere! The race is before you. It's a marathon, not a sprint. Many people start with good intentions, but only a few finish. The scripture says, "Let us throw off everything that hinders and the sin that so easily entangles. And let us run with perseverance the race marked out for us" (Heb 12:1).

The game of life must be played, but it's your choice how you play it. Will you keep the rules? Will you prepare? Will you participate? Will you persevere? If so, you will be a winner!

And that's our prayer for each of you as you go out into the world!

I Have Finished My Course!

2 Timothy 4:7

At graduation we honor those who have finished a task. Scripture says God finished one stage of creation: "Thus the heavens and the earth were finished, and all their multitude. And on the seventh day God finished the work that he had done, and he rested on the seventh day from all the work that he had done" (Gen 2:1–2). Graduates should be commended for finishing one stage of their education. Jesus was serious about finishing what you start. He said, "No one who puts a hand to the plow and looks back is fit for the kingdom of God" (Luke 9:62).

He told stories that ridiculed folks who bit off more than they could chew and didn't complete their projects: "For which of you, intending to build a tower, does not first sit down and estimate the cost, to see whether he has enough to complete it? Otherwise, when he has laid a foundation and is not able to finish, all who see it will begin to ridicule him, saying, 'This fellow began to build and was not able to finish'" (Luke 14:28–30).

Over and over he said, "My food is to do the will of him who sent me and to complete his work" (John 4:34).

"I glorified you on earth by finishing the work that you gave me to do" (John 17:4).

His last words included this point. "When Jesus had received the wine, he said, 'It is finished.' Then he bowed his head and gave up his spirit" (John 19:30).

Paul also emphasized finishing: "But I do not count my life of any value to myself, if only I may finish my course and the ministry that I received from the Lord Jesus, to testify to the good news of God's grace" (Acts 20:24).

"I have fought the good fight, I have finished the race, I have kept the faith" (2 Tim 4:7).

Henry Ford was once asked, "How can I become a success?" Ford replied, "Finish what you start!"

Ford learned this lesson early in his career. When he began work on his first automobile, he worked long but exciting hours in a little brick building behind his home. Such enthusiasm overtook him that he found it hard to take time out to eat or sleep. Before he had completed his first car, however, he became acutely aware that he could build an even better car.

He was so sure of the need for improvements that the thrill and enthusiasm for his first car began to lessen. Why spend all that time finishing a car he already knew was inferior? Still, something inside him forced him to continue, to focus his total energy on the first car and finish what he had started, before he allowed himself to fantasize about a second car.

As it turned out, Ford said he learned even more about how to improve the second car by finishing every detail of his original car. If he had given in to the temptation to quit building the first car, he may never have made any car at all.

Many people strive to be perfectionists, but the completionists usually accomplish more in life.

Why do so many people fail in life?

I. Some People Fail Because They Hook On to Stationary Objects.

These people often exert a lot of effort and stay unbelievably busy but still accomplish nothing.

There's a story about a bar hopper who'd had one too many. He got into a boat and rowed hard all night long. When daylight broke, he was exhausted but triumphant. "I must have really gone a long way," he thought. Unfortunately, when he checked his progress, he found out that the boat had been securely tied to the dock. He was still in the very same place. All that time and energy were wasted.

Are our occupations and avocations in areas that "get us somewhere," or do we expend our time and energy in vain?

What holds you back? What dock are you fastened to? Do you blame your past for your failures? Do you say, "I can't succeed because of my lousy parents, my poor childhood, my lack of opportunity"? If so, those are your docks. You're tied, and you'll never get anywhere.

Since you can't reverse history, wallowing in regret is useless. You must throw out the excess baggage that is holding you back, shift gears, and commit to action.

Once, a writer became ill. She was afraid she'd never finish the book she was writing because she could only lie flat on her back and work half an hour a day. Nevertheless, she finished that book and wrote others. She said she was encouraged to try because a friend had said, "Perhaps you can't row fifty miles in one day. But maybe you could row five miles each day for ten days."

When our choice is between the hard and the easy, between giving up or going on, remember that five miles a day may be a struggle, but if it's in the right direction, it can accomplish wonders.

Untie yourself from that stationary object and work smarter, not harder. Remember: It's not how much you do but what you accomplish that matters.

II. Some People Fail Because They Get Stuck on Circular Treadmills.

These also expend effort. They go to work and come home. They get up, and they go to bed. They go through the motions of life, but for what?

Once, a little old lady attended her first county fair. She spent her small hoard of coins carefully, but an acquaintance finally convinced her to take a ride on a merry go round. Reluctantly, she gave the operator her money and sat down. After about five minutes the music stopped, and she was told to get off. Furiously, the woman reacted, "I paid my money. I got on. I rode around and around, and I got off right back where I started from!"

What a parable of life. We pay our money in the form of precious time and energy. We get on and ride around and around, and then retirement or death puts us off the treadmill. We find that we're right back where we started from. Is this inevitable? Is this all there is?

The meaning of success is different for each one of us. If we go against our unique identities and are not true to ourselves we won't be successful no matter what we do.

Get off the circular treadmill. Realize that efficiency isn't enough. We need fulfillment.

III. Some People Fail Because They Follow Dead-end Paths.

They start down a road that seems promising, but it narrows and narrows until at last insurmountable barriers stop all progress. At this point the travelers must either retrace their steps or stand at the barricades and mark time, pretending to march forward.

Once, a city resident was lost in the country. He approached a native to get some directions. "Can I take this highway?" he asked. "Well, yeah! You can take it," said the mountaineer, "but it won't get you nowhere! Pretty soon this highway turns into a road, then the road turns into a lane, then the lane turns into a pig trail, and finally it stops at a cliff!"

Are we on such dead-end streets?

You only have one life. Make it count! Don't hook on to a rock and row all night for nothing. Don't allow yourself to be held back by past ties and traditions.

Don't pay your money to get on a "merry go round" and just go around in circles. Don't live just to eat and sleep.

Don't go down a dead-end street and then spend your time retracing your steps or standing and marking time!

Cut loose from entanglements. Head for the open sea. Plot an effective course toward your goal. Choose paths that promise ever-widening possibilities in the future.

If you do, at the end of your life, you will be able to say with the Apostle Paul, "I have fought the good fight, I have finished the race, I have kept the faith" (2 Tim 4:7).

Just Say "Nope!"

In today's world of drugs, promiscuity, and crime, there's one vital word that every young person needs to learn and use. That word is nope! Let's use this word as an acrostic to identify four dangerous excuses.

N Means Nobody Will Know I Did It.

That's not true! The scriptures say that God will know: "For human ways are under the eyes of the Lord, and he examines all their paths. The iniquities of the wicked ensnare them" (Prov 5:21–22).

An old joke says, "Three things keep us moral: a strong character, high principles, and an eyewitness." But it's what we do when no one's looking that counts.

When Abraham Lincoln was urged to cut a corner because "no one would know," he said, "You're wrong. I'd know, and I have to sleep with myself!"

Once, when Joseph was a slave in Egypt, his master's wife grabbed his coat and said to him, "'Lie with me!' But he left his garment in her hand, and fled and ran outside" (Gen 39:12).

Now, it would have been easy to say, "Nobody will ever know. I'll just go along and later deny my sin," but Joseph said, "NOPE!"

"Nobody will know I did it" is not a valid excuse because both God and you will know! Scripture says, "The LORD looks down from heaven; he sees all humankind. From where he sits enthroned he watches all the inhabitants of the earth" (Ps 33:13–14).

David said, "For I know my transgressions, and my sin is ever before me" (Ps 51:3).

So when you are tempted to do something you know is wrong, just say "NOPE! That's not for me!"

O Means Once Won't Hurt!

This is not a valid excuse. Scripture says, "Wisdom is better than weapons of war, but one bungler destroys much good" (Eccl 9:18).

Once, the three Hebrew children were in a dangerous predicament. The king had made a strict decree, saying, "Whoever does not fall down and worship will be thrown into a furnace of blazing fire. Shadrach, Meshach and Abednego answered the king, 'O Nebuchadnezzar…our God whom we serve is able to deliver us from the furnace of blazing fire and out of your hand.…

But if not, be it known to you, O king, that we will not serve your gods and we will not worship the golden statue that you have set up" (Dan 3:11, 16–18).

Now, it would have been so easy to say, "Once won't hurt. Just a quick prayer, a bending of the knee, a little bow. It won't mean a thing." That's like saying, "Just one cigarette, just one beer, just one drug experience. It won't matter."

But when we're tempted to say "Once won't hurt," let's remember this scripture: "For whoever keeps the whole law but fails in one point has become accountable for all of it" (Jas 2:10).

So when you're tempted, just say "NOPE!"

P Means People Made Me Do It.

That's peer pressure!

For some reason we don't always want to take personal responsibility. We're like the two little boys caught fighting. When the teacher asked what happened, each one tearfully declared, "It all started when he hit me back."

Scripture says, "Do not enter the path of the wicked, and do not walk in the way of evildoers. Avoid it; do not go on it; turn away from it and pass on" (Prov 4:14–15).

They say good deeds and success have a thousand fathers, but mistakes and failures are orphans.

"People made me do it" is not a valid excuse because you are responsible for you! Scripture tells us that every person is responsible for his own sin (see Deut 24:16b).

Moses once faced a life-altering decision. He could have been Pharaoh, ruler of Egypt, but the scriptures say, "By faith Moses, when he was grown up, refused to be called a son of Pharaoh's daughter, choosing rather to share ill-treatment with the people of God than to enjoy the fleeting pleasures of sin. He considered abuse suffered for the Christ to be greater wealth than the treasures of Egypt, for he was looking ahead to the reward" (Heb 11:24–26).

There was probably pressure from his adoptive mother and his associates. It would have been so easy to say "People made me do it. I had no choice," but instead Moses said "NOPE!"

The scripture says, "My child, if sinners entice you, do not consent" (Prov 1:10).

So when you're with friends who dare you to drink or take drugs or engage in promiscuous behavior, just say "NOPE!

E Means Everyone Else Is Doing It!

That's the myth of "safety in numbers."

Mobs and riots and lynchings have been justified by this mentality, but we're not lemmings. We don't have to jump off the cliff simply because the rest of our species does. The animals in the story "Chicken Little" all shouted, "The sky is falling! The sky is falling!" and blindly followed each other into the fox's den.

The scriptures say, "My child, if sinners entice you, do not consent. If they say, 'Come with us, let us lie in wait for blood; let us wantonly ambush the innocent'; my child, do not walk in their way, keep your foot from their paths" (Prov 1:10–11, 15).

"Everyone else is doing it" is not a valid excuse because you are a majority of one! The scripture says, "You shall not follow a majority in wrongdoing" (Exod 23:2).

So when you are tempted to go along with the crowd in immoral or illegal or harmful activities, just say "NOPE!"

There is only one safeguard against evil companions: Just stay away from them!

Once, Daniel faced a difficult decision. The king ordered his men to eat and drink certain foods that were wrong for a Hebrew. Now, it would have been so easy to say, "Everybody else is doing it. I should go along in order to get along." Besides, they say, "When in Rome, do as the Romans do." But Daniel said, "NOPE!"

When we're tempted to say "Everybody else is doing it," let's remember these scriptures: "You shall not follow a majority in wrongdoing" (Exod 23:2). Paul said, "Each of us will be accountable to God" (Rom 14:12).

So when you're tempted, just say "NOPE!"

Young people, bad habits start early, and they start small. A slip here, a compromise there—soon we're trapped into addictions and dangerous habits and destructive behavior.

When Jesus was tempted three times, he said, "NOPE! NOPE! NOPE!"

When you have to make tough decisions and withstand group pressure, don't say, "Nobody will know" or "Once won't hurt" or "People made me do it" or "Everybody else is doing it." Instead, remember this scripture: "No testing has overtaken you that is not common to everyone. God is faithful, and he will not let you be tested beyond your strength, but with the testing he will also provide the way out so that you may be able to endure it" (1 Cor 10:13).

Your parents used to say "No" for you. But when you are an adult, you must learn to say "NO!" for yourself. And you must stick with it!

If you have to get up early tomorrow for class, then the answer to a late-night party needs to be "No!"

If a guy doesn't treat you like a lady, the answer to his second date invitation should be "No!"

If your friend drinks and then asks you to go for a ride, your answer must be "No!"

Now, saying, "No!" does not mean you hate or reject somebody. It simply means "I don't choose to go along with what you want to do!" Learning to use this little word is a big step toward integrity and maturity.

"No" doesn't have to be said rudely, but it needs to be said assertively, especially when you are being pressured. So, young people,

> In a world of crime and dope,
> There's no better word than "NOPE!"
> To succeed and learn to cope,
> There's no better word than "NOPE!"
> If you want to live with hope,
> There's no better word than "NOPE!"
> —Maralene Wesner

Winning the Game of Life

Everybody likes to win. From wars to football games, we celebrate victories. From graduations to job promotions, we glory in successes. Paul was using the language of an athletic contest when he said, "I press on toward the goal for the prize of the heavenly call of God in Christ Jesus"(Phil 3:14).

There are many kinds of triumphs. Some promote selfishness, and some promote the good of all. When we are truly connected to our fellow men and women, we are no longer trapped in the "I win/you lose" position.

The inability to grasp this reality causes so much heartache. "I win/you lose" causes divorce and family violence. It drives wedges between parents and children. It destroys businesses and churches. It threatens to be the final words spoken in a nuclear disaster.

There is an old story about some men in a boat heading toward land. One man suddenly starts boring a hole in the bottom of the craft. When challenged, he retorts angrily, "This is none of your business. I'm boring this hole under my seat!" He doesn't realize that such problems are everybody's business. All the people in the boat will sink together.

Life is like that. In a small world, my business is your business, and your business is my business. In a small world, if I win, we all win, and if I lose, we all lose. So what leads to universal victories? What determines ultimate success? What ensures a triumphant finish that benefits everyone?

Let's analyze the winning ingredients in the game of life.

I. Knowledge

We must know the fundamentals. Once, when his team was behind and performing badly, a coach walked into the locker room at halftime and began his lecture. "Gentlemen," he said, "let's get back to the basics." Then, reaching down for a nearby pigskin, he held it up and continued, "Boys, this object is a football."

Yes, a player must know the basics of the game and how to fill his position. He must know where the goalposts are and how to get there. Certainly, this is true of the church. Hosea said, "My people are destroyed for lack of knowledge" (Hos 4:6).

For spiritual knowledge it's important to understand the Bible. It contains directions on how to live. It explains how we may enter eternal life. It tells of the Holy Spirit who will guide us. The Bible can keep us from becoming arrogant when we succeed, from being disappointed when we fail, and from being distressed when things go wrong.

The Bible is a source of comfort and joy. It contains countless examples of the strengths and weaknesses of men and women through the centuries from which we may learn. Unfortunately, fewer people read and know the scriptures today than ever before. According to answers received by researchers, Sodom and Gomorrah were thought to be lovers; "Mary and Joseph" was a play written by Shakespeare; the exodus was a motion picture. Only a third of those surveyed knew who delivered the Sermon on the Mount.

Gallup, who did the poll, concluded, "We revere the Bible, but we do not read it.... We are a land of hypocrites who fight to put the Ten Commandments in courthouses and classrooms but can't even name them. We believe in God, but we don't know him."

What if ball players didn't know the rules and couldn't recognize the goal line? They'd never win a game. That's why Bible study and worship and prayer are so important. We must have knowledge.

II. Discipline

This is the key ingredient in anything we do. Peter says, "support...knowledge with self-control" (2 Pet 1:5–6).

Working hard and working smart are still requirements of achievement, and this is nowhere more true than in the church. Solomon said, "Like a city breached, without walls, is one who lacks self-control" (Prov 25:28).

Mary Lou Retton recalled her many years of disciplined training, which resulted in an Olympic gold medal in gymnastics. She said, "When I'd come home from school, as a kid, instead of going out to play, I'd put on a pair of leotards and go to the gym. I worked out when others dated. I exercised while others watched TV. I ate vegetables while others ate ice cream. I missed social activities to get my rest. Still, people say, 'How lucky I am!' They don't know all the work that went into it."

The writer of Ecclesiastes said, "Whatever your hand finds to do, do with your might" (Eccl 9:10).

The problem for most Christians is that they do not consistently give their best. Many are content to do just enough to get by. If we make an effort or if we measure up to our neighbors, we feel okay.

Unfortunately, it's not okay! What if ball players never practiced and disregarded all good health principles? They'd never win a game. That's why self-control and determination and hard work are important. We must have discipline.

III. Cooperation

There are a lot of coaches with good ball clubs who know the fundamentals and have plenty of discipline, but they still don't win games. To be successful, groups must work together. Each player has to be thinking about the next guy and saying to himself, "If I don't block that man, my teammate is going to get hit. I have to do my job well so that he can do his."

The difference between mediocrity and greatness is determined by the feeling the guys have for each other.

Most assuredly, this is true in the family, the church, and the community. Jesus said, "I give you a new commandment, that you love one another. Just as I have loved you, you also should love one another" (John 13:34).

A British sailor said years ago that the most terrible naval battle he ever fought occurred one night when his ship mistook another British ship for the enemy. He said, "Many sailors were killed and wounded, and both vessels suffered heavy damage. When daylight came, we learned of our tragic blunder when we saw the Union Jack flying from both masts. We saluted each other and wept bitterly."

Today, we call such incidents "friendly fire," but it's still deadly.

Sometimes Christians commit the same error. They cause church splits and hard feelings. They criticize other denominations and denounce each other. Such in-fighting destroys everyone. If we insist upon having our own way in every situation, we may ultimately "win" only to realize it's really a tragic loss.

What if every football player was out to protect himself and gain the glory at the expense of his teammates? They'd never win a game. That's why communication and tolerance and compromise are so important. We must have cooperation.

IV. Optimism

Positive thinking is essential. Players must think victory, dream victory, and believe victory.

This also applies to the church. Paul said, "May the God of hope fill you with all joy and peace in believing, so that you may abound in hope by the power of the Holy Spirit" (Rom 15:13).

Hope gives life. Once, a soldier was court-martialed and dishonorably discharged from the army of a foreign country. Strangely enough, he was not discharged for treason, desertion, or sleeping at his post of duty. Instead, he was accused of being a discourager. He did nothing more than go among his fellow soldiers with pessimistic words and negative criticism. He broke the spirit and tore down the morale of his unit. His presence was more of a hindrance than a help to accomplish the task at hand.

It's alarming how often this same situation prevails in churches and businesses. People may not violently fight against the program. They just mingle and complain. They voice skepticism concerning the plans and goals of the organization. In a very real sense, they are discouragers.

Sometimes it's difficult to detect such action because it can be accomplished in very subtle ways. Often, there are too many critics and not enough workers. The discourager may not really intend to be an enemy and a traitor, but he is.

What if the players and cheerleaders and managers all sat around saying, "They have a better team. We're no good. We can't make a goal."? They'd never win a game. That's why positive thoughts and healthy attitudes and cheerful words are so important. We must have optimism.

V. Perseverance

We have to finish the game. A brilliant first half isn't enough. We must have players who'll be in there until the final whistle is blown. We can't just run until we experience a little pain or get a little tired or feel a little discouraged. No! We must be committed to the end. Above all, this kind of commitment is needed in the church.

Jesus said, "The one who endures to the end will be saved" (Matt 24:13).

Paul said, "So let us not grow weary in doing what is right, for we will reap at harvest-time, if we do not give up" (Gal 6:9).

Many great things are never accomplished because we quit too soon. Many lessons are never learned because we quit too soon. One of Andrew Jackson's boyhood friends said, "When we wrestled, throwing Andy was no problem. Why, I could throw him nine times out to ten, but the problem was, he wouldn't stay throwed!"

That's the hallmark of a winner—he won't stay throwed! He always gets up and tries again.

What if all the players on a football team quit as soon as they encountered resistance or saw their competitors score a touchdown? They'd never win a game. That's why persistence and patience and faithfulness are so important. We must have perseverance.

A winning coach knows that you can move mountains one shovelful at a time. The Great Wall of China took hundreds of years to construct, but it was built one stone at a time. The great pyramids of Egypt were constructed one block at a time.

That's how you win. You have knowledge. You have discipline. You have cooperation. You have optimism. And above all, you have perseverance. You keep digging. You keep chipping. You keep trying, knowing that in the end you are going to be a winner.

Independence Day

I Don't Know, and I Don't Care!

Amos 5:24; 6:1

Someone asked, "What are the two greatest problems in America today?" A typical citizen answered, "I don't know, and I don't care!"

"That's exactly right!" the questioner replied. "It's ignorance and apathy."

Our democracy is threatened by the complacency of its citizens more than it is by the hostility of its enemies. Americans are more intrigued with personal gossip than with public issues. Americans care more about who wins the Super Bowl than they do about who wins the highest offices in our land.

Our ignorance, our apathy, and our unbelievable sense of priorities are illustrated by the reaction in 1941 when Pearl Harbor was bombed. Thousands of people called radio stations to complain that their regular programs were interrupted in order for that momentous news to be broadcast.

Many people drop out of the democratic process because they feel insignificant. They say, "My opinion doesn't matter. My vote won't make any difference!" But recent close elections have proved it does.

As patriotic Americans, do we know enough, and do we care enough? A wise man said, "Patriotism is not singing 'The Star-Spangled Banner' and saluting the flag! It's discovering truth and implementing justice."

I. Ignorant People Can't Remain Free!

Solomon said, "The wise lay up knowledge" (Prov 10:14).

Hosea said, "My people are destroyed for lack of knowledge" (Hos 4:6).

Jesus said, "You will know the truth, and the truth will make you free" (John 8:32).

Free individuals must make up their own minds on the basis of information. This is especially true for those of us who live in a democracy. A congressional aide shared the story of handling calls and correspondence related to a major bill in Congress. Over ninety percent of those contacting that office had demanded a specific course of action. But that representative disregarded those calls and letters. He voted differently because most of the people contacting that representative had their facts wrong. They knew nothing about the legislation. They were just expressing emotion and responding to propaganda.

In fact, propaganda is so prevalent today that we must be alert and critical. Factual information should be obtained before we make decisions. We're too prone to make snap judgments and take illogical stances. For instance, in the New Haven study, a huge majority favored a "free press," yet over a third said they wouldn't permit a newspaper to criticize America. Now, these two attitudes are mutually exclusive. The press is either free or it's not! We can't pick and choose.

Also, we must avoid temporary fixes. Shortsighted remedies are like the little old lady who made some curtains. When they were finished, she hung them, and to her dismay, they were three inches short. "Oh, my!" she said. "What will I do? I don't have any more cloth. Aha!" she exclaimed. "I know what to do. I'll take them down and cut three inches off the top and sew it on the bottom. Then they will be long enough."

Now, don't laugh! That same process is used every day in politics and business. They lower income taxes and raise sales taxes—cutting off one end and sewing it on the other. They add $1,000 to the price of a car and give a $500 rebate and you think you've gotten a bargain. That's cutting it off one end and sewing it on the other. Doing away with educational grants and then supporting the unskilled through welfare is likewise unproductive.

Christians must point out and eliminate such inequities and foolishness in their government. We have a promise: "If any of you is lacking in wisdom, ask God, who gives to all generously and ungrudgingly, and it will be given you" (Jas 1:5).

That's important because we desperately need intelligence in complex matters. It's been said that "smart rascals haven't done our world as much harm as ignorant saints!"

Unfortunately, narrow evaluations of character are shortsighted. The fact that a candidate goes to church or abstains from alcohol doesn't necessarily make him an excellent political statesman. Many misguided German Christians supported Adolf Hitler at the beginning of his rule because he didn't smoke or drink.

We have to understand what is at stake in legislation and foreign policy. We must not be unduly swayed by emotional rhetoric and patriotic propaganda.

How much do we really know about America? Are we depending on biased commentators and ignorant informers to tell us the truth about our country? Do you know what is really happening in the lives of families in our country?

Every day in our country, teenagers get pregnant; babies die before their first birthday; children are wounded or die from gunshots; teenagers die by suicide; young people are arrested for abusing drugs, drinking, or drunk driving; teenagers drop out of school; children are abused or neglected; children run away from home; children see their parents divorce; children are placed in adult jails. Much of this is due to ignorance and could be prevented with proper information and education. We need to know! Ignorant people can't remain free!

II. Apathetic People Can't Remain Free!

Solomon said, "Do not withhold good from those to whom it is due, when it is in your power to do it" (Prov 3:27).

James said, "But be doers of the word, and not merely hearers who deceive themselves" (Jas 1:22).

Jesus said, "And whoever gives even a cup of cold water to one of these little ones...truly I tell you, none of these will lose their reward" (Matt 10:42).

America needs concerned people. There are many special-interest groups that crusade for one issue, but few that champion a broad array of issues and problems that afflict our society. We must see the deeper causes and the broader implication of these causes. We must take the long view rather than the immediate gratification. In 1900 Theodore Roosevelt said, "This country will not be a good place for any of us to live in unless we make it a good place for all of us to live in." Today we should alter this to say, "This world will not be a good place for any of us to live in unless we make it a good place for all of us to live in."

Some vacationers charted a yacht. A day into the journey, it sprang a leak and began to take on water. The captain decided the passengers would need to help bail water to keep the ship afloat. While passing out buckets, he came across one tourist still lying on his bunk. "Hey, fellow!" the captain said. "How about giving us a hand? This boat is in danger of sinking!"

The man peered over the side of his bunk at the dry floor and replied, "Why should I be worried?" he whined. "There's no water under my bunk!"

A lot of us are like that guy. We don't help others because the problem is not yet affecting us. "After all," we reason, "it's really their problem, not mine. Why stick my neck out?"

Unfortunately, this sense of apathy is evident in our country. So we wait until it's too late before we realize that action is called for. Too many of us are like Moses at the burning bush when God called him to carry out a difficult task. He said, "I have never been eloquent, neither in the past nor even now that you have spoken to your servant; but I am slow of speech and slow of tongue... please send someone else" (Exod 4:10, 13).

Most of us know somebody should do something, but we want that somebody to be somebody else. If we want to change society, to transform it for Christ, we must truly live as free persons. We must act in an informed manner, out of a depth of concern. And each of us can do that! We are more important than we think we are. Just one person can make a difference. Just one vote can make a difference!

Yes, America has many problems, and two of the greatest are ignorance and apathy. Theodore Roosevelt warned, "The things that will destroy America are: prosperity-at-any-price; safety-first instead of duty-first; the love of soft living; and the get-rich-quick theory of life." He could be describing us today! To a great extent, our objectives have become financial success and personal pleasure

A democracy demands individuals who know and individuals who care. One citizen said, "I asked, 'Why doesn't somebody do something?' Then I realized that I was somebody."

As Christians, it's our duty to avoid ignorance and apathy!

Free to Be Me

Galatians 5:1, 13-14

Freedom is an awesome blessing, but it's also an awesome responsibility. Unfortunately, we don't usually appreciate it until we've lost it! Ask a POW or a kidnapped victim or a prison inmate what they crave most. The answer will be freedom.

Most of us enjoy the gift of freedom every day. But are we grateful for that gift, and do we use our freedom in a productive way?

I. Freedom to Think

The freedom to think is almost absolute because no government or authority can regulate or control our thoughts. Nevertheless, our thoughts can be influenced by processes of brainwashing, conditioning, and propaganda. Evil leaders and destructive groups have caused tragedies like the Jim Jones massacre and the Jewish Holocaust by manipulating the thinking process of normal individuals. They do this by isolating men and women from their normal support groups, by censoring all other viewpoints and giving only one side of an issue. They present misleading information. They take quotes from other perspectives out of context. They repeat their doctrines and teachings over and over in a hypnotic manner, until their victims lose their ability to think reasonably and evaluate objectively.

To protect our freedom to think, we must be alert to brainwashing and propaganda techniques. We must not fall for scams. If something sounds too good to be true, it's probably false. As they say, "The only free cheese is in the mousetrap."

We must reject false teachings, and we must keep our own thoughts pure and positive. According to Jesus all evil originates in the thoughts. He said, "It's what comes out of a person that defiles. For it is from within, from the human heart, that evil intentions come: fornication, theft, murder, adultery, avarice, wickedness, deceit, licentiousness, envy, slander, pride, folly" (Mark 7:20–22).

The writer of Hebrews said, "The word of God…is able to judge the thoughts and intentions of the heart. And before him no creature is hidden, but all are naked and laid bare to the eyes of the one to whom we must render an account" (Heb 4:12b–13).

Paul said, "Finally, beloved, whatever is true, whatever is honorable, whatever is just, whatever is pure, whatever is pleasing, whatever is commendable, if there is any excellence and if there is anything worthy of praise, think about these things" (Phil 4:8).

We must use our freedom to think logically.

II. Freedom to Speak

The freedom to speak has a few limits. We're not free to slander or incite to riot or to threaten our government. We're not free to call 911 and give a false report. We're not free to deceive customers and clients in advertisements and commercials. But in most instances we can express our views and opinions openly without fear of arrest or punishment. That means we are the ones who are accountable for our comments and verbal messages.

As Christians we have even further restraints on what we should say. James gave excellent advice and warnings concerning our speech. He said, "If any think they are religious, and do not bridle their tongues but deceive their hearts, their religion is worthless" (Jas 1:26).

James also explains the power and importance of words with several illustrations. He said,

> For all of us make many mistakes. Anyone who makes no mistakes in speaking is perfect, able to keep the whole body in check with a bridle. If we put bits into the mouths of horses to make them obey us, we guide their whole bodies. Or look at ships: though they are so large that it takes strong winds to drive them, yet they are guided by a very small rudder wherever the will of the pilot directs. So also the tongue is a small member, yet it boasts of great exploits. How great a forest is set ablaze by a small fire! And the tongue is a fire. The tongue is placed among our members as a world of iniquity; it stains the whole body, sets on fire the cycle of nature, and is itself set on fire by hell. For every species of beast and bird, of reptile and sea creature, can be tamed and has been tamed by the human species, but no one can tame the tongue—a restless evil, full of deadly poison. With it we bless the Lord and Father, and with it we curse those who are made in the likeness of God. From the same mouth come blessing and cursing. My brothers and sisters, this ought not to be so. (Jas 3:2–10)

We must use our freedom to speak respectfully.

III. Freedom to Act

If you were the only inhabitant of the earth, you would have total freedom to act. But as the old saying goes, "Your freedom ends where my nose begins." That means we are free to do things that only concern ourselves, but we are not free to do things that hurt others. As an individual I am free to be stupid. I am free to make silly mistakes. I am free to fail. But I am not free to harm other people with my stupidity and mistakes. I am not free to cause them to fail.

It's hard to draw the line. People may say, "It's my life. If I want to smoke or drink or engage in reckless behavior, I'm free to do so." But no man is an island. Almost all of one person's actions, directly or indirectly, affect someone else. Therefore, we have laws that curtail our freedoms. We must stop at a red light. We must observe speed limits. We must buy liability insurance.

But Christians have further limits. We are no longer our own. Paul said, "Do you not know that your body is a temple of the Holy Spirit within you, which you have from God, and that you are not your own? For you were bought with a price; therefore glorify God in your body" (1 Cor 6:19–20).

If we belong to Christ, that takes away our freedom to injure ourselves. We don't have the freedom to harm other people. We don't have the freedom to bring dishonor to God, our church, and our witness. Paul said, "But take care that this liberty of yours does not somehow become a stumbling block to the weak" (1 Cor 8:9).

He also said, "For you were called to freedom, brothers and sisters; only do not use your freedom as an opportunity for self-indulgence, but through love become slaves to one another" (Gal 5:13).

Jesus definitely required Christians to do much more than keep the letter of the law. He told us to go the second mile. "And if anyone wants to sue you and take your coat, give your cloak as well; and if anyone forces you to go one mile, go also the second mile" (Matt 5:40–41).

Now, it's natural to be selfish. It's human nature to look out for "number one." But rising above your humanity is what Christianity is all about. We must use our freedom to act responsibly.

America can only remain free if its citizens are willing to think logically, speak respectfully, and act responsibly.

An immigrant recounted memories of her coming to America. They were Russian refugees in Austria. American soldiers there treated them with dignity and respect. When orders came for the family to return to Russia, an American officer listened to her mother's fears that upon return the communists would send her to Siberia and us children to an orphanage. The officer intervened, and they were allowed to remain in Austria. Three years later, they were reconnected with some relatives and were able to immigrate to America. The mother for the first time could vote, and the family could live truly free—worshipping as they chose, pursuing higher education, coming and going as they pleased!

Too often we don't appreciate our freedom because we've always had it.

As Americans let's be grateful. And as Christians let's be even more grateful. Paul said, "For freedom Christ has set us free. Stand firm, therefore, and do not submit again to a yoke of slavery" (Gal 5:1).

How to Realize Our Responsibilities

People yell for their rights, but they seldom yell for their responsibilities. Many of us are like a certain reluctant football star. It seems the players on the opposing team were absolutely ferocious. They humiliated man after man. Then the coach said to the quarterback, "Give the ball to Willie." But instead he gave it to John, and there was no gain. Again, the order came: "Give the ball to Willie!" Again, it was given to another player with no gain. Finally, the irate coach called the quarterback out and demanded, "Why didn't you give the ball to Willie?" "Sir," the quarterback replied, "Willie said he didn't want the ball!"

Sometimes we don't want the ball. We avoid duties and obligations. We're too lazy or too immature or too timid to accept our responsibilities. Paul said, "Each of us will be accountable to God" (Rom 14:12).

Later, Paul added that as Christians we are not only personally accountable for ourselves; we are also, to a certain extent, responsible for others. He said, "We who are strong ought to put up with the failings of the weak, and not to please ourselves" (Rom 15:1).

Unfortunately, most people don't want to bear their own burdens, much less the burdens of others. "Let George do it" has become our national motto. This doesn't work. Passing the buck, denying, evading, and blaming are wrecking our families. It's also wrecking our economy. It's wrecking our country, as politicians lie to get elected and citizens "vote their pocketbooks" rather than their convictions.

So how can we realize our responsibility?

I. We Must Recognize Our Responsibilities.

God said, "I know your works; you are neither cold nor hot. I wish that you were either cold or hot. So, because you are lukewarm, and neither cold nor hot, I am about to spit you out of my mouth" (Rev 3:15–16).

To be lukewarm is to be apathetic and evasive. It's to take the easy way, even if it means ducking our responsibilities.

Jesus said, "Stay awake and pray that you may not come into the time of trial; the spirit indeed is willing, but the flesh is weak" (Matt 26:41). To stay awake and pray means to be alert and aware. Jesus knew the human personality is invariably tempted to be weak and selfish. He knew the human personality is prone to justify its behavior. Nevertheless, excuses won't do. A concert violinist started to play his opening number, but a string broke. He kept right on playing with only three strings. When he finished, the applause called him back again and again. Many never knew he had played under a handicap, and the ones who did know admired his performance all the more.

You see, there is not a person in the world who has everything. Just when we think things are okay, a string always breaks. The question is: Will we quit, or will we play on with those three strings we have left?

Some people say, "Well, I had a bad childhood" or "I've experienced bad luck. Therefore, I can't be blamed; I can't quit that bad habit; I can't be productive." Some people avoid hard tasks and cop out when the going gets rough. But the world needs reliable citizens, and God expects us to be dependable witnesses. So we must use what we have and recognize our responsibilities.

II. We Must Acknowledge Our Responsibilities.

John said, "Love has been perfected among us in this: that we may have boldness on the day of judgment, because as he is, so are we in this world" (1 John 4:17).

We can't deny our responsibility. We are here to be God's agents.

We are taking Jesus's place here on earth. We are God's eyes and ears and hands and feet. If we don't carry out his purposes, they won't get done. During the Christmas season many years ago, a ragged boy stood looking in a beautiful store window. But his eyes were not on the mechanical toys or other bright things that a boy would normally be looking at. Instead, he was looking beyond these things to a very warm pair of boots sitting in the window. You see, this little boy was standing there with nothing on but a very thin shirt, thin pants, and no coat. His feet were wrapped in rags. Just then, a limousine pulled up in front of the store, and a chauffeur opened the door for a finely dressed lady. She noticed the little boy as she started inside. Immediately, she took his hand and led him into the store and began to outfit him. First of all, she got him a warm coat, then a cap with flaps to pull down over his ears, some stockings, and at last that beautiful pair of warm fur-lined boots in the window. As she dressed the little waif, he looked up at her with tears in his eyes and said, "Ma'am, are you God's wife?" She smiled and said, "No, I'm not his wife, but I am one of his daughters."

This woman saw a need she could fill and recognized her responsibility. As sons and daughters of God, we must exemplify his attitudes and carry out his purposes. There is much to be done here on this earth.

III. We Must Accept Our Responsibilities.

Jesus said, "Why do you see the speck in your neighbor's eye, but do not notice the log in your own eye?" (Matt 7:3).

Blaming others is totally nonproductive. Most people find it much easier to see the flaws in others than to see the flaws in themselves. Once, a preacher concluded a scathing sermon on the sin of swearing. As the service ended and the worshipers were filing out the door, the first one was a woman. Never suspected of using foul language, with an angry face she exclaimed, "I will never darken this door again." Before the astonished preacher could recover, another said, "Pastor, if I had known you were listening last week, I would have been more careful of my language." A third said, "You should have come to me privately about this rather than telling it to the whole church."

Then the real culprit came by—the one the preacher had been targeting. With an innocent smile he shook the preacher's hand and said, "Pastor, that was what I call a real sermon. You certainly did put it on them today!"

You see, people seldom recognize their own sins. They say, "He did it; she did it; they did it; the devil made me do it! It wasn't my fault! I'm not to blame!" These words don't solve problems, but they've been around since the very beginning of time. We admire a George Washington, who said "I did it" when asked who chopped down the cherry tree. So we must accept our responsibilities rather than blame others.

When we have knowledge and opportunity, we are responsible; the more we know and the more opportunities we have, the more responsible we are. Jesus said, "From everyone to whom much has been given, much will be required; and from the one to whom much has been entrusted, even more will be demanded" (Luke 12:48).

In light of this scripture, Americans are at risk. We have more schools and more churches and more Bibles and more resources than anyone in the history of the world. But what have we done with them? We have violence and drugs and divorce and abuse. Also, in light of this scripture, leaders are at risk. Ministers and teachers and politicians who have chosen places of influence have an enormous responsibility to be righteous.

Paul said, "So then, each of us will be accountable to God" (Rom 14:12).

Your first step is to recognize—rather than evade—your responsibilities. Right now, analyze your choices and decisions: Are they selfish or unselfish? Do you ever rationalize and excuse yourself? Do you say, "It's not my problem; let someone else do it"?

Your next step is to acknowledge—rather than deny—your responsibilities. Right now, think of all your own strengths and skills and abilities. Think of all your blessings and opportunities. Consider your behavior. Are you using what you have? Are you fulfilling all your duties? Are you investing your talents in service to others, or are you burying them?

Your final step is to accept your responsibilities—rather than blame others. Right now, are you ready to let "the buck stop" at your door? Are you prepared to correct your own inadequacies and failures? Are you able to admit your mistakes? Are you willing to do your part with enthusiasm?

Today we are facing critical decisions and enormous problems. As citizens, as Americans, as Christians, we must do our duty and realize our responsibilities.

Keeping America Great

We live in a great nation. We didn't build it. We may not deserve it. But we have the responsibility of preserving it.

The test of life is not what you do, but what you do with what you have to do with.

Jesus tells of a king who called in three of his servants. To one servant he said, "I'm going to give you five talents," to another "two," and to another "one." Then he said, "I'm going out of the country for a long journey, and I want you to be stewards of the talents I have given you."

The king came back many months later and called the one to whom he had given the five talents and discovered that he had taken those five talents and developed them into ten. The other one, to whom he had given two talents, had developed them into four. And he said to each, "Well done! You are a good and faithful servant. You have been faithful over a few things; I want you to be master over many. Enter into your kingdom."

However, the man who had the one talent reported that he had very carefully protected his talent. He had buried it! Now he was prepared to give that talent back to the king. The king said, "I expected you to do something with this." And he turned to his guards and told them to take this man's talent and give it to the man who had developed ten talents. And he said, "For to all those who have, more will be given, and they will have an abundance; but from those who have nothing, even what they have will be taken away" (Matt 25:29).

God gave us many talents. He gave us arms and hands and feet and a head to use. If we put our arm in a sling for a year, we'll lose the use of it. Fish in dark caves become totally blind. In life, if we don't use our talents, we'll lose them.

Our forefathers had a great dream, a unique dream! They envisioned a nation of liberty, a nation of opportunity.

We doubt America. We have inflation, recession, deficits. We have problems at home and overseas.

So what? This nation has always had problems! We've had Watergate! We've had the Vietnam War! But we're a nation of strength, a nation of commitment. We have survived crises in the past, and we will survive the crises of the future.

History shows that our forefathers had a common goal; they had discipline and dedication; they had foresight and vision. The constitution they wrote is a masterpiece.

Where is that spirit of America? Where are the Nathan Hales and the Patrick Henrys? We still have them. If this nation is challenged, we will rise to meet that challenge.

So how can we keep America great?

I. We Need Motivation.

People are our finest resources. People can do anything. Alfred Sloan, the founder of General Motors, said it best, "Take my money, take my machines, take my buildings, take my land; just leave me my people and we'll come back as strong as ever."

There are many examples from history of people who overcame great odds and handicaps to make their mark in this world! We can do it too! It has been done by those whose difficulties and handicaps are greater than ours. Beethoven, one of the great composers of the world, was deaf! John Milton, who wrote Paradise Lost, was blind.

Several years ago, an athlete was injured so seriously in a car accident that the doctors said he would never walk again. Yet that man came back and within one year became the U.S. Open champion. His name, Ben Hogan.

Not too long ago, a man bored with retirement used the talents God gave him to start a new business. Today we enjoy Colonel Sanders' Kentucky Fried Chicken.

If we have the desire, God will give us the opportunity. As Emerson wrote, "Man must always reach beyond his grasp, or what's a heaven for?" It's our obligation to utilize our talents.

Worrying about our problems never helps! One of the great sins of life is worry. No doomsayer ever accomplished anything. Let's be thankful for life! Let's do the best we can with what we have!

To keep America great, we need motivation.

II. We Need Participation.

We have a great nation! It's the country that survived the Civil War, two world wars, numerous depressions, many recessions, the assassination of three presidents, and the resignation of one. America will survive! It has an inner strength, but it needs our help, our interest, and our support.

As Christians we have an obligation to believe in America and to do our part. People must not just sit around waiting for the government to do something. This is our nation. We are in charge. We can make a contribution. We can change things.

Outside of our own health, family, and faith, there is nothing more important than our government. It directly affects our lives. We have to get a driver's license before we can drive a car. We have to get a building permit before we can build a home. We have to get a business permit before we can operate a business. Every time we stop at a stop sign, we are feeling the effects of government.

This country is worth not just fighting for, but working for and living for! If this nation is to fulfill its heritage, we must make the same kind of commitment that our forefathers made many years ago. It's time we stopped complaining and started serving. Opportunities are unlimited for those who will reach out and take them.

George Bernard Shaw said it best: "People sit around and blame their problems on circumstances. I do not believe in circumstances; I believe the people who get on in this life are the people who find the circumstances they want, and if they can't find them, they make them!"

We're not going to build this country by wringing our hands. We must participate. We have too many lessons from history—Athens, Rome, and others who lived on the glories of their past instead of meeting the challenge of their future. Christianity tells us we are expected to shape that future!

To keep America great, we need participation.

III. We Need Appreciation.

Don't talk about "the good old days." Today is "the good day." We have more of everything than any generation has ever had. This nation is the wealthiest on earth. Our nation is the breadbasket of the world. We publish more books than the rest of the world put together. We have more churches, more symphonies, more operas, and nonprofit theaters than any other nation.

They say the eighth wonder of the world is the great American system of freedom and liberty. But they also say the ninth wonder of the world is the average American's lack of appreciation for that system.

We should be proud to be Americans! We have the freedom to criticize our government and seek changes. We've walked on the moon! We've helped make the earth safe from disease! We've transplanted human hearts! We feed half the world! We've elevated the dignity of man! We have magnified faith in God. We can choose our destiny and then work to achieve it.

To keep America great, we need appreciation.

Yes, we live in a great country. We are free! We are Americans. God bless America. On election day, do your part! Vote!

The Star-Spangled Banner
2 Chronicles 7:14

"The Star-Spangled Banner," written by Francis Scott Key during the War of 1812, starts with a question. Marooned on a British ship, Key watched helplessly as it attacked Ft. McHenry near Baltimore, Maryland. Through the night's bombardment, he looked for the American flag flying over the fort: "Oh, say, can you see, by the dawn's early light …?"

Is that banner still streaming? Think about it. Every time you sing our national anthem, you're asking a question. And that's the question we must ask today: Is our flag still flying over the land of the free? Is our flag still flying over the home of the brave? Is our flag still flying over a nation that is free, courageous, and righteous? And what can we do to ensure that our flag will continue to fly over such a nation?

I. We Must Be Vigilant and Observant.

We must commend and encourage politicians and legislators when they are right, but we must be equally willing to criticize and protest when they are wrong.

When Peter and the apostles were confronted with a conflict between laws and authorities and their own conscience, they said, "We must obey God rather than any human authority" (Acts 5:29).

Unfortunately, there aren't many scriptures about patriotism and citizenship because there were no democracies in Bible times. There were no elections. Individuals had few rights and even fewer choices about government. Monarchs and dictators were absolute rulers. Kings made all the decisions. Emperors determined the regulations and laws.

Even so, we do find some biblical guidelines concerning our responsibilities. God gives us a formula to ensure that our country will continue to live up to its potential. "If my people who are called by my name humble themselves, pray, seek my face, and turn from their wicked ways, then I will hear from heaven, and will forgive their sin and heal their land" (2 Chron 7:14).

Today, our land needs healing. There is too much ignorance and gullibility. There is too much brainwashing and shallow conditioning. There is too much hostility and polarization. Too many citizens and politicians are looking out for their own selfish interests rather than trying to discover what's good for the whole population.

If Christians demand the right to give a public prayer in the classroom, then they must be prepared to allow the Muslim, the Buddhist, and every other group the same right. If we force Jehovah's Witnesses to pledge allegiance to the flag or Quakers to engage in combat, then we must be willing to compromise our precious principles when the time comes that we aren't in the majority position. In short, all people's faith must be respected, not just ours.

We must think before we jump on popular political bandwagons. For instance, if we teach the Genesis creation story of Adam and Eve in public schools, we must be prepared to study other creation stories. Every culture has its mythological explanation of the origin of life, and all of them have a right to teach theirs if the Christian teaches his.

You see, we can't always impose our will, even if it's actually best. We must persuade and influence, but not coerce. Some well-meaning people would force their religious beliefs on the multitudes. This has led to inquisitions and persecutions. Burning someone at the stake to save his soul is never justified. Passing "blue laws" to force people to worship on Sunday is not effective.

We must realize that Christians are the salt and light in a nation. We set the moral tone. Solomon said, "Righteousness exalts a nation, but sin is a reproach to any people" (Prov 14:34).

II. We Must Be Active and Involved.

Paul said, "Do not lag in zeal, be ardent in spirit, serve the Lord" (Rom 12:11).

A patriot doesn't just wave the flag. Instead, he works and votes and writes his congressman. A patriot doesn't just sing "God Bless America" and recite the Pledge of Allegiance. He knows words are cheap. So he walks his talk.

A patriot doesn't attack, ridicule, and vilify those who disagree with him. Benjamin Franklin said, "A patriot isn't swayed by emotion and propaganda. Instead, he uses his God-given intelligence and makes sensible decisions." A wise man said, "Those who corrupt the public mind are just as evil as those who steal from the public purse."

A patriot doesn't spend his time pointing fingers at the opposition. Instead, he knows the only person he can change is himself!

Jesus said, "In everything do to others as you would have them do to you; for this is the law and the prophets" (Matt 7:12a).

Christians must do what is good, but that's often hard to determine. Knowing what is good for the moment isn't enough. A present good can be a future evil. Persistence and patience are essential.

The most important attribute of any statesman or citizen is farsightedness. In matters of government, we must develop a historical perspective. Choosing the difficult but permanent solutions over the easy but temporary ones requires strength of character and moral courage. Expediency may win elections, but it doesn't serve civilization.

Paul said, "Be steadfast, immovable, always excelling in the work of the Lord, because you know that in the Lord your labor is not in vain" (1 Cor 15:58).

III. We Must Be Informed and Dedicated.

Many leaders have fought and died to ensure the freedom of speech and voting rights we have today. One reason America is great is because it was settled by courageous people. Optimists came here from all over the world with faith in the future. They left the fearful and anxious pessimists on the docks of Europe and Asia.

Too often, we sacrifice values on the altar of convenience. After signing the Constitution of the United States, one signer said, "Well, folks, I think we've given you a democracy. Now, if you can just manage to keep it."

The sacred torch of freedom has now been passed down to us. We must not drop it! Paul said, "Guard what has been entrusted to you" (1 Tim 6:20).

Our nation has had great blessings. It has wonderful opportunities. It has great potential for good. Let's not waste these resources. Jesus said, "From everyone to whom much has been given, much will be required; and from the one to whom much has been entrusted, even more will be demanded" (Luke 12:48b).

That's so true of America. We must not fail.

America's greatest strength is its dedication to human rights. We do care about people. The poem at the base of the Statue of Liberty says:

> Give me your tired, your poor,
>
> Your huddled masses
>
> Yearning to breathe free.
>
> The wretched refuse of your teeming shore,

Send these, the homeless,
Tempest-tossed to me.

I lift my lamp beside
The golden door.
—Emma Lazarus

America is great, and we must do all we can to keep her great. Our national anthem asks three important questions: Is our flag still flying over the land of the free? Is our flag still flying over the home of the brave? Is our flag still flying over a nation of justice and righteousness?

This is the question we must ask today as we celebrate our nation's birthday. Are the "stars and stripes" still waving over a land of the free? Are the "stars and stripes" still waving over the home of the brave? Are the "stars and stripes" still waving over a nation that practices righteousness?

Today, as Christians we must work to make sure that we will be able to answer Francis Scott Key's question with a resounding "Yes!"

Halloween

Removing Your Mask
2 Corinthians 3:17, 18

Kids wear masks at Halloween to fool people. Robbers wear masks to hide their identity. Actors wear masks to play a role.

In fact, the word hypocrite means, "One who wears a mask." Jesus had a lot to say about masks: "So whenever you give alms, do not sound a trumpet before you, as the hypocrites do in the synagogues and in the streets, so that they may be praised by others. Truly I tell you, they have received their reward. ... And whenever you pray, do not be like the hypocrites; for they love to stand and pray in the synagogues and at the street corners, so that they may be seen by others. Truly I tell you, they have received their reward. ... And whenever you fast, do not look dismal, like the hypocrites, for they disfigure their faces so as to show others that they are fasting. Truly I tell you, they have received their reward" (Matt 6:2, 5, 16).

Later, he warned, "Beware of false prophets, who come to you in sheep's clothing but inwardly are ravenous wolves" (Matt 7:15).

Jesus didn't like for individuals to appear to be different than they really are. He said, "Woe to you, scribes and Pharisees, hypocrites! For you clean the outside of the cup and of the plate, but inside they are full of greed and self-indulgence. ... Woe to you, scribes and Pharisees, hypocrites! For you are like whitewashed tombs, which on the outside look beautiful, but inside they are full of the bones of the dead and of all kinds of filth" (Matt 23:25, 27).

In fact, Jesus hated pretense above all things. He wants us to be honest. He wants us to be real.

We don't have to guess what a two-year-old child is feeling. Children don't hide anything. What they need is obvious. What they believe is obvious. What they enjoy is obvious. What they know is obvious. What they can do is obvious.

But as adults we are different: We have learned to mask what's inside. We put on brave faces. We put on game faces. We put on poker faces. We put on happy faces.

These masks have been designed to hide our true selves. Too often when we say "I'm fine," we'd really like to confess, "I'm frustrated, irritated, nervous, and exasperated!"

But Paul tells us we don't have to pretend. We can be free to reveal our own faces. He said, "Now the Lord is the Spirit, and where the Spirit of the Lord is, there is freedom. And all of us, with unveiled faces, seeing the glory of the Lord as though reflected in a mirror, are being transformed into the same image from one degree of glory to another; for this comes from the Lord, the Spirit" (2 Cor 3:17–18).

A salvation experience allows us to discover and reveal our true selves. When we know we are loved and forgiven and created in God's image, we can remove our masks and let our own unique personalities emerge. Masks are no longer required. We are finally free to be who we were meant to be.

Let's take off our masks, uncover our faces, and be the person God created. To do this:

I. We Must Discover Our Needs.

What are you willing to sacrifice time and energy in order to obtain? What are your greatest frustrations and aggravations? What conditions are necessary for you to be comfortable and productive?

For example, a fish needs to live in water; an eagle needs to fly in the air; prairie dogs need holes in the ground; dogs need bones, and cows need grass. Like these animals, each of us has different needs, and these needs are legitimate. Some people need adventure and excitement; some people need accomplishments and results; some people need security and order; some people need stability and peace.

Trying to be popular by pretending to like what our friends like is wrong. Trying to be successful by pretending to want what our associates want is wrong! It's okay to be different.

Each of us deserves to have our deep needs met. Paul said, "And my God will fully satisfy every need of yours according to his riches in glory in Christ Jesus" (Phil 4:19).

You can't be real unless you are honest about your needs.

II. We Must Analyze Our Values.

What principles do you live by? What do you believe in? What moral convictions do you hold?

Joshua states his values by saying, "Now if you are unwilling to serve the Lord, choose this day whom you will serve, whether the gods your ancestors served in the region beyond the River or the gods of the Amorites in whose land you are living; but as for me and my household, we will serve the LORD" (Josh 24:15).

Micah also listed three values that were important to him. He said, "To act justly and to love mercy and to walk humbly with your God" (Mic 6:8).

All mature, successful people have values they live by. They have moral standards and beliefs that shape their lives. Paul expressed his belief system, saying, "For to me, living is Christ" (Phil 1:21).

You can't be real unless you are honest about your values.

III. We Must Consider Our Interests.

What gets your attention? What do you like to talk about? What do you enjoy doing?

Some people love music; some love art; some are interested in science. Others gravitate toward crafts or mechanics. Some enjoy city life; others enjoy nature. It's okay to have special interests that others may not share. The writer of Ecclesiastes said, "There is nothing better for mortals than to eat and drink, and find enjoyment in their toil" (Eccl 2:24). "Likewise all to whom God gives wealth and possessions and whom he enables to enjoy them, and to accept their lot and find enjoyment in their toil—this is the gift of God" (Eccl 5:19).

You can't be real unless you are honest about your interests.

IV. We Must Inventory Our Knowledge.

What facts have you acquired? What information have you learned? What educational credentials have you earned?

Everyone is knowledgeable about something, but no one knows everything. We can all learn from each other. Many illiterate individuals are extremely intelligent and wise about life. Some people have academic knowledge, or "book learning." Others have practical information, called "street smarts." Both are important. Solomon said, "for wisdom is better than jewels, and all that you may desire cannot compare with her" (Prov 8:11).

You can't be real unless you are honest about your knowledge.

V. We Must Develop Our Skills.

What special abilities do you have? What achievements are easy for you? What projects have you completed?

Everyone has talents and gifts, but no one can do everything. Einstein wasn't a good artist. Many musicians are poor mechanics. Paul said, "We have gifts that differ according to the grace given to us" (Rom 12:6a). "Now there are varieties of gifts, but the same Spirit" (1 Cor 12:4).

Peter said, "Like good stewards of the manifold grace of God, serve one another with whatever gift each of you has received" (1 Pet 4:10).

You can't be real unless you are honest about your skills.

If you discover your real needs, your real values, your real interests, your real areas of knowledge, and your real skills and areas of expertise, then you will begin to understand who you really are. What's more important, you'll realize that you're a significant and worthwhile person. Remember our text: "Now the Lord is the Spirit, and where the Spirit of the Lord is, there is freedom. And all of us, with unveiled faces, seeing the glory of the Lord as though reflected in a mirror, are being transformed into the same image from one degree of glory to another; for this comes from the Lord, the Spirit" (2 Cor 3:17–18).

From the beginning we were created to reflect God. The scripture says, "So God created humankind in his image, in the image of God he created them" (Gen 1:27).

We can only reflect God by removing our masks.

When you realize your worth as God's child and find your niche in God's overall plan and begin to fulfill your purpose, then you'll be able to live an authentic life and you'll never have to wear a mask again.

The only way we can be authentic witnesses for God here on this earth is to be our true selves.

An advertisement featured a pretty blonde. She was being used to hype a school of modeling. The caption said, "Be a model...or at least look like one." That's pretense. God never said, "Be a Christian...or at least look like one."

Jesus never said, "Truly I say to you, if you do not have a religious bumper sticker, you cannot be my disciple" (see Luke 14:27). He never said, "Be careful to appear righteous before men. If you do, you will have a reward from your father in heaven" (see Matt 6:1). He never said, "Whoever wants to become great among you must wear a pious smile" (see Mark 10:43). He never said, "I tell you the truth, unless you act like you're born again, you cannot see the kingdom of God" (see John 3:3).

That's what masks do. We may know all the rules of "religiosity." We may know what not to do, or at least what not to get caught doing. We may go through the outward motions of looking like what we think a Christian should look like. We may fool some people, but we don't fool God. He sees through counterfeit Christianity and knows when we're wearing masks.

God is depending on each one of us to reflect his love and truth here on earth. That requires honesty.

Once, some missionaries went to a remote village. Natives listened patiently as the preachers tried to explain Jesus's love. When they described how Jesus lived for what he could give rather than for what he could get, the villagers nodded their heads and smiled. When they spoke about how he even forgave his enemies, the old villagers looked at each other with knowing eyes. Finally, one of them spoke: "We know this man. Your 'Jesus' once lived here."

The missionaries shook their heads and explained that he had actually lived many years ago and many thousands of miles away.

"No! No! He lived and died right here," the natives insisted. "Follow us, and we'll show you his grave."

The missionaries followed the natives to an old cemetery. There they stopped at a headstone carved with the name of a Christian medical missionary—a man who felt God had led him to that village. He had lived and died there. His existence was unknown to the world. Yet he had been so Christlike that the natives believed him to be Jesus of Nazareth.

Every Christian is such a missionary. The scripture says, "As he is, so are we in this world" (1 John 4:17).

You are God's representative in your own corner of the world. In your school, your home, your job, you influence many people that no one else can. If you will take off your mask and be authentic, real, honest, and faithful, others will be able to see Christ in you.

The Real Me
Luke 19:1-9

On Halloween we wear pretend masks and pretend costumes. We try to fool people about who we are. Of course, at Halloween it's just a game. Unfortunately, most of us do this every day, and it's not a game. We express emotions we don't feel. We say things we don't mean. We do things we don't want to do. We paste fake smiles on our faces. We agree to things we don't believe in. We con others in order to be popular. Such pretense is not good for us, and it's not good for anybody else. So, today, let's find "the real me" under the masks and costumes.

Jesus helped several Bible characters find themselves, and the surprising results are miraculous.

I. An Extremely Wealthy Man with a High Government Position

He had a nice home, good food, and all the luxuries of life. But several factors combined to make him feel inadequate.

In that day, respectable Jewish society ostracized fellow Jews who collected taxes for Rome. Not only did these traitors collaborate with the hated foreigners, but most were also guilty of using their position to extort extra money for themselves. As chief tax collector, Zacchaeus administered this extortion process in an entire district.

Also, this Publican was very short. Others probably ridiculed his size, and this, plus his unethical lifestyle, made him defensive and miserable.

As he searched for meaning, possessions became his coping mechanism, and selfishness took over. Sometimes greed develops because we are searching for meaning. As we try to fill our emptiness, things are simply substitutes.

After Zacchaeus climbed a tree in order to see the Lord in the crowd, he faced his moment of decision. Fortunately, Jesus saw the real Zacchaeus beneath the false trappings. The scripture says, "When Jesus came to the place, he looked up and said to him, 'Zacchaeus, hurry and come down; for I must stay at your house today.' So he hurried down and was happy to welcome him" (Luke 19:5–6)

Now, Zacchaeus had been hated, ridiculed, and rejected. His neighbors even criticized Jesus for befriending him. The scripture says, "All who saw it began to grumble and said, 'He has gone to be the guest of one who is a sinner.'" (Luke 19:7).

Of course he was a sinner. We all are! But when Jesus gave him acceptance, his life changed. His mask came off, allowing his real goodness and generosity to become apparent. He became a great benefactor, saying, "Look, half of my possessions, Lord, I will give to the poor; and if I have defrauded anyone of anything, I will pay back four times as much" (Luke 19:8). Jesus responded, "Salvation has come to this house" (Luke 19:9).

II. A Woman with Terrible Personal Problems

She couldn't seem to achieve a lasting relationship, as one after another of her marriages collapsed. Abuse and infidelity had worn her down, and now she didn't even bother with a legal arrangement. Instead, she simply lived with men. She was the victim of gossip, and the respectable women no longer associated with her. Coming to the village social center every day was a nightmare.

Then, one day, this Samaritan woman was confronted with her moment of decision. When she came to the well, an unexpected stranger began a conversation with her. In that culture, men didn't speak to women in public and certainly not to immoral women.

An even greater barrier existed in this case. The man was a Jew, and she was a Samaritan. These two groups had decades of racial animosity. The Samaritans had intermarried with pagans, and the Jews had even rejected their help in rebuilding the temple.

In fact, most Jews totally avoided this region of Palestine, but Jesus sat down to rest at Jacob's well while his disciples went into the village to buy food. Soon, this woman came to draw water.

Again, Jesus saw the real woman beneath the false trappings. He spoke to her and said, "'Those who drink of the water that I will give them will never be thirsty. The water that I will give will become in them a spring of water gushing up to eternal life.' The woman said to him, 'Sir, give me this water, so that I may never be thirsty or have to keep coming here to draw water'" (John 4:14–15).

His friendliness and total lack of judgment changed her life. Her mask came off, allowing her real depth and concern to become apparent. She became a witness to others. The scripture says, "Then the woman left her water jar and went back to the city. She said to the people, 'Come and see a man who told me everything I have ever done! He cannot be the Messiah, can he?'" (John 4:28–29).

III. A Man Who Had a Criminal Past

He was a lawbreaker and a detriment to society. Eventually, he was caught and sentenced to death. He knew he was guilty and admitted his illegal activities and sins. For him, life was over. It seemed to be too late for another chance. There was no time for a retrial or a pardon. The execution was already being carried out. Then, suddenly, the thief on the cross was confronted with his moment of decision.

In speaking of the thieves on the crosses, a theologian said, "The scripture records the last-minute conversion of one thief to give us hope, but it records only one such conversion, so we won't be presumptuous."

Now, on this occasion there were two thieves who had been exposed to the same sights and sounds. They were equally culpable, yet one joined in the mockery of Jesus, and the other responded and believed. The penitent thief expressed an amazing faith. At the darkest hour, when all seemed lost, even to Jesus's closest followers, this man reached out in faith. Now, it's likely that he had a limited experience with religion. He certainly didn't have the advantage of observing Jesus's miracles or hearing him preach. He probably understood little of Jesus's mission, but he realized that Jesus was the savior, and he saw himself as a dying sinner.

When the thief asked to be remembered in Christ's coming kingdom, Jesus promised he would be with him in paradise on that very day.

Jesus saw the real man beneath the false trappings. The scriptures say, "Then [the thief] said, 'Jesus, remember me when you come into your kingdom.' Jesus answered him, 'Truly I tell you, today you will be with me in paradise'" (Luke 23:42–43).

The Lord didn't hesitate or condemn or require apologies. His total unquestioned forgiveness and promise of hope changed the criminal's life. His mask came off, allowing his deep faith to become apparent. He now had hope and a future.

So what masks are you wearing? What costumes are you wearing? What problems are you denying? What sins are you hiding? You may fool others. In fact, you may even fool yourself. But Jesus doesn't see masks and costumes. He sees the real person.

What does Jesus see when he looks at you?

According to an old Greek legend, Helen of Troy was kidnaped and taken to a distant city. She suffered from amnesia and became a prostitute in the streets. She didn't know her name, her birthplace, or that she was of royal blood.

Meanwhile, back in her homeland, friends didn't give up. A loyal admirer believed she was alive and kept looking for her.

One day when he was wandering through the streets of that strange city, he saw a dirty, wretched woman wearing tattered clothes. But something about her seemed familiar. When he approached and asked, "What is your name?," she shook her head in confused bewilderment.

After a closer look he gasped, "You are Helen! You are Helen of Troy! Do you remember?"

She looked up at him in astonishment. "You are a queen," he explained. Gradually, the fog seemed to clear, and a sense of recognition came to her face. Helen discovered her lost self, and she put her arms around her old friend and wept.

Fortunately, because of his belief in her, Helen was restored to health and once more became the queen she was born to be.

That's an analogy of the gospel. God says, "You are valuable! You are important! You are loved! No matter how you look, what you've done, or how far you've fallen, the real you is a child of God, created in the image of God. Don't cover it up with artificial masks and costumes."

If Jesus could forgive and accept a hated greedy traitor like Zacchaeus, who lied and cheated his neighbors, he can forgive and accept you and me! If Jesus could forgive and accept an immoral individual like the woman at the well, who had numerous husbands and assorted live-in lovers, he can forgive and accept you and me! If Jesus could forgive and accept a robber and convicted criminal like the thief on the cross, who had no time left for baptism or good deeds, surely he can forgive and accept you and me.

That is the gospel! That is the good news! That is the message Jesus wants us to proclaim!

How to Get Rid of Your Ghosts
Philippians 3:12-14

Mark Twain once remarked, "I don't believe in ghosts, but I'm afraid of them!" Sometimes there is a gap between our thoughts and our feelings. All of us have ghosts from our past. We have regrets, sorrows, failures, losses, defeats, disappointments, problems, and sins that haunt us. But if we dwell on them, they will destroy us.

The scriptures are full of people with destructive ghosts:

A psalmist said, "When my soul was embittered, when I was pricked in heart, I was stupid and ignorant; I was like a brute beast toward you" (Ps 73:21–22).

Isaiah said, "Woe is me! I am lost, for I am a man of unclean lips, and I live among a people of unclean lips" (Isa 6:5).

Jeremiah said, "Let us lie down in our shame, and let our dishonor cover us" (Jer 3:25a).

Ezekiel said, "Our transgressions and our sins weigh upon us, and we waste away because of them" (Ezek 33:10).

David was a man with a lot of ghosts in his past. He had committed adultery. He had lied. He had murdered. At this particular low point in his life, he said, "For my life is spent with sorrow, and my years with sighing; my strength fails because of my misery, and my bones waste away" (Ps 31:10).

Later, he said, "For I know my transgressions, and my sin is ever before me" (Ps 51:3). Yet he dared to believe he could be restored. In a heartfelt prayer he asked to be cleansed. He said, "Wash me thoroughly from my iniquity, and cleanse me from my sin. Purge me with hyssop, and I shall be clean; wash me, and I shall be whiter than snow" (Ps 51:2, 7).

He asked for purity: "Create in me a clean heart, O God, and put a new and right spirit within me" (Ps 51:10).

He asked for joy, "Let me hear joy and gladness; let the bones that you have crushed rejoice. Restore to me the joy of your salvation, and sustain in me a willing spirit" (Ps 51:8, 12).

Because God forgave him and destroyed the ghosts of his past, he promised to be a witness to others, saying, "Then I will teach transgressors your ways, and sinners will return to you" (Ps 51:13).

Even though he had sinned, David was known as a man after God's own heart. The scripture says, "The LORD has sought out a man after his own heart; and the Lord has appointed him to be ruler over his people" (1 Sam 13:14).

Peter also had ghosts. He denied Jesus at a crucial moment. He let him down. He did the unthinkable. In fact, he did what he had just declared he would never do. When they were discussing the situation earlier, Peter had said, "Lord, I am ready to go with you to prison and to death!" (Luke 22:33).

At that time Peter was sincere, but talk is cheap. Later, when push came to shove and the danger was real, he reacted differently. The scriptures say, "Then they seized [Jesus] and led him away, bringing him into the high priest's house. But Peter was following at a distance. When they had kindled a fire in the middle of the courtyard and sat down together, Peter sat among them. Then a servant-girl, seeing him in the firelight, stared at him and said, 'This man also was with him.' But he denied it, saying, 'Woman, I do not know him.' A little later someone else, on seeing him, said, 'You also are one of them.' But Peter said, 'Man, I am not!' Then about an hour later still another kept insisting, 'Surely this man also was with him; for he is a Galilean.' But Peter said, 'Man, I do not know what you are talking about!' At that moment, while he was still speaking, the cock crowed. The Lord turned and looked at Peter. Then Peter remembered the word of the Lord, how he had said to him, 'Before the cock crows today, you will deny me three times.' And he went out and wept bitterly" (Luke 22:54–62).

Now, for the rest of his life, don't you imagine that every time he heard a rooster crow, that ghost of denial and disloyalty came forth? Nevertheless, Peter preached a great sermon to thousands and became a respected leader in the early church.

Then there was Paul the Apostle. He had more ghosts in his past than most. He had persecuted the Christians. He had tried to demolish the early church. He had participated in the stoning of Stephen. But listen to what he said, "Beloved, I do not consider that I have made it my own; but this one thing I do: forgetting what lies behind and straining forward to what lies ahead" (Phil 3:13).

Paul was able to put his ghosts behind him. Paul not only put his ghosts behind him; he used them as motivation. In several of his letters, he emphasized freedom from guilt. He wrote, "Blessed are those who have no reason to condemn themselves" (Rom 14:22b).

He had total confidence in the Lord's power to forgive and redeem. He said, "Blessed is the one against whom the Lord will not reckon sin" (Rom 4:8).

Then he said, "For freedom Christ has set us free. Stand firm, therefore, and do not submit again to a yoke of slavery" (Gal 5:1).

David, Peter, and Paul had every reason for regret, yet they went on to accomplish great things. They got rid of their ghosts by accepting God's grace.

Jesus said, "Just so, I tell you, there will be more joy in heaven over one sinner who repents than over ninety-nine righteous persons who need no repentance" (Luke 15:7).

Repentance is a good thing, a necessary thing. Those who repent are honest in admitting and dealing with their mistakes. Repentance includes insight, confession, and change.

The writer of Hebrews describes insight and dedication. He said, "Let us approach with a true heart in full assurance of faith, with our hearts sprinkled clean from an evil conscience and our bodies washed with pure water" (Heb 10:22).

Solomon advocated confession. He said, "No one who conceals transgressions will prosper, but one who confesses and forsakes them will obtain mercy" (Prov 28:13).

Later, John said, "If we say that we have no sin, we deceive ourselves, and the truth is not in us. If we confess our sins, he who is faithful and just will forgive us our sins and cleanse us from all unrighteousness" (1 John 1:8–9).

Ezekiel explained repentance. He said, "Repent and turn from all your transgressions; otherwise iniquity will be your ruin. Cast away from you all the transgressions that you have committed against me, and get yourselves a new heart and a new spirit!" (Ezek 18:30–31).

Peter also emphasized change. He said, "Repent therefore, and turn to God so that your sins may be wiped out" (Acts 3:19).

Remorse, however, can be nonproductive. Wallowing in guilt and having pity parties is useless. Paul gives an excellent comparison between repentance and remorse when he writes to the church at Corinth. He explains, "Now I rejoice, not because you were grieved, but because your grief led to repentance; for you felt a godly grief, so that you were not harmed in any way by us. For godly grief produces a repentance that leads to salvation and brings no regret, but worldly grief produces death" (2 Cor 7:9–10).

So get rid of your ghosts of regrets, shame, and guilt. Your past is forgiven. David understood this because he had experienced it. He said, "Bless the Lord, O my soul, and do not forget all his benefits—who forgives all your iniquity, who heals all your diseases...who satisfies you with good as long as you live so that your youth is renewed like the eagle's.... The Lord is merciful and gracious, slow to anger and abounding in steadfast love. He will not always accuse, nor will he keep his anger forever.... For as the heavens are high above the earth, so great is his steadfast love toward those who fear him; as far as the east is from the west, so far he removes our transgressions from us" (Ps 103:2–3, 5, 8–9, 11–12).

After failing twice in the 1988 Olympic speed-skating race, Dan Jansen went to a sports psychologist, who helped him pay more attention to the mental aspects of skating. In 1994 Jansen had more confidence than ever. He had set a 500-meter world record just two months before. But during this race Jansen fell. He was shaken. His coach immediately advised, "Put the 500 behind you. Stop reliving it. Start preparing for the 1000-meter race!"

Dan had always considered the 1000-meter race to be his weakest event. But it was his last chance for an Olympic gold medal. As the race began, Jansen said, "I just seemed to be sailing along." But then he came within an inch of stepping on a lane marker. Still, he didn't panic. He raced on and established a new world-record time that won him the gold medal.

Once, Northwestern University had a thirty-four-game losing streak. It had set a national collegiate football record. But a new coach, Dennis Green, said, "I can't worry about what happened in the past. I can't shoulder that responsibility. I think that the team will do much better if we think about the upcoming games we can win, rather than about the past games that we lost."

We can learn a lesson from Coach Green's words: We can't go back and undo our record either. At this point in our lives, we must leave our past mistakes and failures to God.

We must get rid of our ghosts. We must follow Paul's advice when he said, "Forgetting what lies behind and straining forward to what lies ahead, I press on toward the goal for the prize of the heavenly call of God in Christ Jesus" (see Phil 3:13–14).

Which Mask Do You Wear?

Romans 12:1-2

We hear a lot about multiple personalities. All of us have conflicting elements. Paul felt this internal confusion and expressed it dramatically: "I do not understand my own actions. For I do not do what I want, but I do the very thing I hate. Now if I do what I do not want, I agree that the law is good. But in fact it is no longer I that do it, but sin that dwells within me. For I know that nothing good dwells within me, that is, in my flesh. I can will what is right, but I cannot do it. For I do not do the good I want, but the evil I do not want is what I do. Now if I do what I do not want, it is no longer I that do it, but sin that dwells within me. So I find it to be a law that when I want to do what is good, evil lies close at hand. For I delight in the law of God in my inmost self, but I see in my members another law at war with the law of my mind, making me captive to the law of sin that dwells in my members. Wretched man that I am! Who will rescue me from this body of death? Thanks be to God through Jesus Christ our Lord! So then, with my mind I am a slave to the law of God, but with my flesh I am a slave to the law of sin" (Rom 7:15–25).

Such spiritual, mental, and emotional stress makes us miserable. It destroys our productivity. It will eventually kill us.

Let's examine these different personalities and different masks.

I. The Person We See

Few of us are totally objective about our own characteristics. Sometimes we're too hard on ourselves. We know our faults and weaknesses. We are aware of our secret guilts and fears. We feel unworthy and insecure. In underestimating our importance, we deny the value of God's supreme creation and destroy our own self-esteem.

Sometimes we're too easy on ourselves. We make excuses for our failures and justify our selfishness. We blame others for our problems and cover up our shortcomings. In overestimating our importance, we run the risk of becoming arrogant and egocentric.

The scriptures give many warnings against such self-deceit. John said, "If we say that we have no sin, we deceive ourselves, and the truth is not in us" (1 John 1:8).

You see, evaluating our real worth and potential is hard. It's always difficult to see the picture clearly if you're inside the frame. That's why the person we see may or may not be an accurate reflection of who we really are.

If you look at a mirror in a fun house, the image you see is not true. It doesn't show you who you really are. The distortion can be misleading. Once, a psychiatrist was counseling a severely depressed patient. He finally said, "I hear there's a performer in town, an extremely funny clown. Why don't you go see him? Maybe he can cheer you up."

"Oh, Doctor," the patient explained, "that won't help. You see, I'm that clown."

Are there phony pretenders living inside us? Do we see ourselves as we really are?

II. The Person Others See

We try to put our best foot forward in public. We even wear masks with our friends. We do this because we feel people would not like us if they really knew all about us. We hide behind protective armor because we're afraid to let our true feelings show. We wear intellectual disguises because we don't think our opinions are valid. Jesus repudiated such false fronts. He said, "Woe to you, scribes and Pharisees, hypocrites! For you clean the outside of the cup and of the plate, but inside they are full of greed and self-indulgence" (Matt 23:25).

Counterfeits are common today. They say a certain fellow bought a mousetrap and put it in his cellar. Since he didn't have any cheese, he cut out a picture of some cheese and put it in the trap. When he went down to check the next morning, he found the picture of cheese had been replaced with a picture of a mouse. You see, one fake leads to another.

Since falseness is so common, the person others see may or may not be an accurate reflection of who we really are. Public opinion is shallow.

There's a lot of posturing and public relations hype in the world. Clothes and status symbols are used to promote candidates and rock stars. People are packaged like perfume and "sold" to a gullible populace.

Do others see us as we really are?

III. The Person God Sees

The scripture says, "the LORD does not see as mortals see; they look on the outward appearance, but the LORD looks on the heart" (1 Sam 16:7).

Jesus said, "You are those who justify yourselves in the sight of others; but God knows your hearts; for what is prized by human beings is an abomination in the sight of God" (Luke 16:15).

We can't fool God. Jesus said, "This people honors me with their lips, but their hearts are far from me" (Matt 15:8).

The psalmist describes a spiritual schizophrenic: "With speech smoother than butter, but with a heart set on war" (Ps 55:21a).

Yes, living in uncertainty is miserable. Trying to perpetuate a sham is futile. Let's be who we are! God loves us that way.

Furthermore, God sees us as potential saints. He sees us as we can be. He sees our possibilities.

God didn't see Abram, the pagan. He saw Abraham, father of a chosen race: "Now the LORD said to Abram, 'Go from your country and your kindred and your father's house to the land that I will show you. I will make of you a great nation, and I will bless you, and make your name great, so that you will be a blessing'" (Gen 12:1–2).

God didn't see Jacob, the crook. He saw Israel, head of a nation: "God said to him, 'Your name is Jacob; no longer shall you be called Jacob, but Israel shall be your name.' So he was called Israel. God said to him, 'I am God Almighty: be fruitful and multiply; a nation and a company of nations shall come from you, and kings shall spring from you'" (Gen 35:10–11).

God didn't see Simon, the liar. He saw Peter, a rock. Jesus said, "Blessed are you, Simon son of Jonah! …you are Peter, and on this rock I will build my church" (Matt 16:17–18).

God didn't see Saul, the murderer. He saw Paul, a committed missionary: "He is an instrument whom I have chosen to bring my name before Gentiles and kings and before the people of Israel" (Acts 9:15).

God believes the best about us. By believing the best, he brings out the best.

Paul said, "I can do all things through [Christ] who strengthens me" (Phil 4:13).

God wants us to let our true, unique nature show forth. Jesus said, "Let your light shine before others, so that they may see your good works and give glory to your Father in heaven" (Matt 5:16).

He didn't say, "Let your pastor's light shine, or some great saint's light shine." He said, "Let your light shine." Each of us brightens dark corners that no one else can reach.

We can truly believe that the person God sees is an accurate reflection of who we really are. When a child is born, something brand new comes into the world. Among all the billions of people, there has only been one of me and one of you. Each of us can do something that no one else can do. Each of us can make a special contribution to the world. Robert Louis Stevenson once said, "To be who we truly are, and to become all we are capable of becoming, is the only end of life."

The psalmist said, "What are human beings that you are mindful of them... you have made them a little lower than God, and crowned them with glory and honor. You have given them dominion over the works of your hands; you have put all things under their feet" (Ps 8:4–6).

Since God sees us as we really are, it's unfortunate that our true self is so often lost among our false selves. Someone said, "That man's reputation wouldn't recognize his character if it met it!"

Is your reputation different from your character? If so, you're not a whole person. The greatest goal of your life should be to find yourself!

Many years ago, an "identification rally" for amnesia victims was scheduled in Paris. Thousands of relatives of missing persons gathered in a great plaza. One by one, the men and women were led to a central platform to speak these words: "Is there anyone here who can tell me who I am?"

That's a universal question. Do you really know who you are? Are there three different persons inside your skin? Who do you see? Who do others see? Who does God see?

It's only when these three merge into one integrated soul that we become truly whole. We don't have to live in a confusion of masks. Jesus came to tell us who we really are. We're sons and daughters of God. He came to tell us where we are. We're here on earth as God's representatives. He came to tell us why we're here. We're here to reflect God's glory and share God's grace with a hurting world.

Are you a multiple personality? Are you a non-person? Are you confused and empty? You needn't remain in that state. Jesus came to give you life! He said, "The thief comes only to steal and kill and destroy. I came that they may have life, and have it abundantly" (John 10:10).

In one scene of the play Godspell, the character Jesus takes a bucket of water, a rag, and a mirror. He goes to his disciples one by one and washes away their painted-on clown faces. Then he holds the mirror up in front of them so they can see themselves as they really are, and then he hugs them. The point is obvious and powerful. We don't have to wear false faces. We don't have to hide our inadequacies. And we don't have to pretend to be something we are not! God loves us and accepts us just as we are! We call that "amazing grace"!

So during this Halloween season, it's okay to have fun with costumes and masks, but don't wear them every day. Instead, be yourself.

Masks

A Children's Sermon

(MATERIALS NEEDED: A variety of masks: happy or funny, sad, scary, etc., for illustration; enough simple masks to give one to each child).

On Halloween we wear things to make us look different. They hide our real faces. They make people think we are someone we're not. They fool people. What are they? (Let children respond.)

Yes! They are masks!

You know, some of us wear a kind of mask at other times too. We cover up our feelings. We say things we don't mean. We are afraid people won't like us if they see us as we really are.

Some of us hide behind silliness and try to get people to laugh.

We hide behind happiness and pretend we are having fun when we're not.

Some of us hide behind sadness and try to get people to feel sorry for us.

Some of us hide behind meanness and try to scare or bully others.

Wearing masks on Halloween is okay, but it's not good to do it all the time. God wants us to be honest, to be free, to be ourselves.

We don't have to hide and pretend. It's all right to show our real feelings, to ask questions, and to act naturally. God loves us as we are!

Jesus said, "This is my commandment, that you love one another as I have loved you" (John 15:12).

So be real!

Children's choir: "Jesus Loves Me!"
Prayer: "God, we thank you for loving us as we are." Amen!

Thanksgiving

An Attitude of Gratitude

A legend tells us that two angels started out to gather up the prayers of mankind. "Let's divide the work today," said one of the angels. "I'll gather the prayers of praise and thanksgiving. You gather the complaints and requests."

At sunset they met again. "Oh," one angel exclaimed, "such a day I've had. This bag didn't begin to hold the complaints and requests. I've had to make three dozen trips. Who would believe that folks could find so much to gripe about?"

"And I," said the other sadly, "I have looked all day long where people seemed to have everything, and I found only this one little 'Thank you.'"

We're an ungrateful lot. Paul said, "[Give] thanks to God the Father at all times and for everything in the name of our Lord Jesus Christ" (Eph 5:20).

"Let the peace of Christ rule in your hearts... And be thankful" (Col 3:15).

Now, the scriptural command to be thankful is as important as the command to be moral, yet how many of us follow it? This commandment, like all of God's commandments, is for our good. What does a spirit of thankfulness do?

I. An Attitude of Gratitude Makes Us Better.

Smiling and laughing make us healthier. Optimism and hope make us more productive. Even so, when it comes to gratitude, most of us are inconsistent. People who narrowly escape an accident are thankful, but what about those who were never in danger? People who lose their job and get another one are thankful, but what about those who never lost their job? People who are very ill and then recover are thankful, but what about those who were never sick?

You see, it's fairly easy to be thankful for avoiding tragedy, but we take normal level times for granted. Paul said, "Be thankful for all things." He meant we're to use the special blessings, the normal times, and even the adversities for good.

One man just out of the hospital prayed this prayer: "Thank you for sickness—not because it is enjoyable, but because it teaches lessons that health cannot teach.

When my skin was hot from fever, I truly appreciated the touch of a cooling hand. When I was dizzy, I came to appreciate gravity, which before had been mostly a nuisance when I lifted objects. When I was hurting, I wasn't interested in the TV evening news. When I was nauseated, I didn't care about the inflation rate. I learned that while you're dealing with sickness or death, things that once seemed so important weren't any more. These lessons help us to establish our priorities."

Happy people are not always thankful, but thankful people are usually happy. That's why an attitude of gratitude makes us better.

II. An Attitude of Gratitude Makes Our Country Better.

Greed is the opposite of gratitude. Greed and selfishness can destroy America. In fact, greed and selfishness can destroy any democracy.

The Pilgrims got no federal aid. No one guaranteed them anything. Their only roads and schools were built by themselves. If they wanted security, they saved or they starved. All these early settlers had was character. All they did was work. All they wanted was self-respect. It's those three traits that made America great.

Democracy is a precious and fragile thing. It only exists until the voters discover that they can vote themselves money from the public treasury. From then on, the majority always votes for candidates promising the most benefits. The average lifespan of the world's greatest civilizations has been two hundred years. These nations have progressed through the following sequence: from bondage to courage, from courage to liberty, from liberty to abundance, from abundance to selfishness, from selfishness to complacency, from complacency to apathy, from apathy to dependence, and from dependence back into bondage again. That's the cycle of greedy people.

Unfortunately, greedy people often get exactly what they say they want, but in the process they lose what they have. In a land of liberty, responsibility is the flip side of freedom. In a land of liberty, the citizens are expected to obey the laws and pay their taxes voluntarily. Patriotism doesn't consist of flag waving. Patriotism consists of positive outlooks and positive actions. That's why an attitude of gratitude makes our country better.

III. An Attitude of Gratitude Makes the World Better.

It does this because as you and I are, so is the world. It's amazing that everyone thinks of changing other people and outer circumstances, but no one thinks of changing himself. An attitude of gratitude would automatically eliminate criticism, gossip, pessimism, and despair. An attitude of gratitude would automatically increase praise, encouragement, optimism, and hope.

Clergyman Edward Everett Hale said it well.

> I am only one, but still I am one.
> I cannot do everything, but still I can do something.
> And because I cannot do everything,
> I will not refuse to do the something that I can do.

Of course, you can't make everything perfect on this earth, but you can do a great deal with what you have. If you observe a lake full of sailboats, you'll notice that each one will be going in a different direction while the wind is blowing in only one direction. How can that be? Well, the answer is very simple. The human beings on those boats adjust the sails. They all use the same set of circumstances, but they use them in different ways. We can use our circumstances for good or for evil.

The same experience can make one person stronger and another weaker. The same sun that hardens bricks, melts butter. What we do with circumstances depends upon the substance of our own makeup.

There's a story about twin boys. One of the twins was an incurable pessimist and the other a perpetual optimist. The problem baffled the parents, so they separated the boys, putting the pessimist in a barn with a beautiful little pony and the optimist in a barn filled with manure. Later, when they went to check, they found the pessimist sitting in a corner sulking. "This horse is gonna mess up the place, and I'll have to clean it!"

Then they found the optimist shoveling furiously at the pile of manure. "What are you doing?" they asked. "Well," the boy answered, not missing a stroke, "with all this manure, there has to be a pony in here somewhere."

You see, a pessimist sees the bad in the good, and an optimist sees the good in the bad.

Horace Greeley was a famous newspaper editor despite his absolutely terrible penmanship. Once, he fired a young man for incompetence and gave him a written letter detailing his deficiencies. Greeley was surprised years later to meet the man and learn that he had become very successful. "How did you manage that, after I fired you?" he asked. The former employee smiled. "Well, I owe it all to your letter of recommendation," he replied. "But that wasn't a letter of recommendation," Greeley snapped. "You know that, and I know that," the man said. "But after carrying that letter in my pocket for months, all that was recognizable was your signature. And that was enough to get me a good job."

Optimism helps us turn misfortune into opportunity. This leads to productivity. That's why an attitude of gratitude makes the world better. We should develop an attitude of gratitude because it makes us better; it makes our country better; it makes the world better.

A very old man said, "If I had my life to live over, I would talk less and listen more. I would invite friends over to dinner even though the carpet is stained and the sofa is faded. I would eat popcorn in the 'good' living room and worry less about the dirt when someone wanted to light a fire in the fireplace. I would burn the pink candle shaped like a rose before it melts in storage. I would sit on the lawn with my children and grandchildren and not worry about the grass stains. I would cry and laugh less while watching television—and more while watching life. I would share more of the responsibilities carried by my partner. I would go to bed when I am sick instead of expecting the earth to disintegrate if I miss a day of work. I would say 'I love you' and 'I'm sorry' more often. But mostly, given another shot at life, I would seize every moment. I would live it; I would enjoy it and never give it back!"

A positive outlook is extremely important. Thankfulness doesn't involve things. Christians don't have to have perfect health and great wealth and unlimited pleasures in order to be grateful. Remember this: "He who has God and everything else, has no more than he who has God and nothing else."

Let's develop an attitude of gratitude.

We Must Be Thankful

1 Thessalonians 5:18

During World War II a soldier was sent to a rest camp after a period of active service. When he returned to his outfit, he wrote a letter to General George Patton and thanked him for the splendid care he had received. General Patton wrote back that for thirty-five years he had sought to give all the comfort he could to his men, adding that this was the first letter of thanks he had ever received.

Most of us show a lack of gratitude. That's because as human beings we're conditioned to notice what's wrong and take for granted what's right. Parents must constantly remind children who have received a gift, "Now what do you say?" As we grow older, we tend to expect the good things of life and seldom thank God, who is the giver of "every good gift and every perfect gift."

That's why we have a day called "Thanksgiving." The best rule is the one given by Paul, "Give thanks in all circumstances" (1 Thess 5:18).

I. We Must Be Thankful for Our Beautiful World.

There's free air and water and skies and sunsets. There's flowers in spring, vegetables in summer, leaves in autumn and snow in winter—so much to see and appreciate.

Once, a blind boy sat on the steps of a building with a hat by his feet. He held up a sign that said: "I am blind; please help." There were only a few coins in the hat.

One man walked by and dropped money into the hat. But then he took the sign, turned it around, and wrote some words. He put the sign back so that everyone who walked by would see the new words.

Soon, the hat began to fill up. A lot more people were giving money to the blind boy. That afternoon, the man who had changed the sign came to check on things. The boy recognized his footsteps and asked, "Were you the one who changed my sign this morning? What did you write?"

The man said, "I only wrote the truth. I said what you said but in a different way." I wrote, "Today is a beautiful day, but I cannot see it."

Both signs told people that the boy was blind. But the first sign simply stated a fact. The second sign reminded people that they were so fortunate to have sight. That's why the second sign was more effective.

The writer of Ecclesiastes said, "[God] has made everything suitable for its time" (Eccl 3:11).

That's why we must be thankful for our beautiful world.

II. We Must Be Thankful for Family, Friends, and Neighbors.

We take our loved ones for granted.

> If I knew this was our last meeting,
> Then I would gladly share your day;
> But since we have so many others,
> I'll just let this one slip away.
>
> I think there'll always be tomorrow
> For us to mend that oversight.
> We always get those second chances
> To hug and finally set things right.
>
> But, still, in case I am mistaken,
> And this one day is all we get,
> I must not be unkind or thoughtless
> And say those things I will regret.
> —Adapted by Maralene Wesner

The writer of Ecclesiastes said, "Two are better than one.... For if they fall, one will lift up the other" (Eccl 4:9–10).

We must be thankful for family, friends, and neighbors.

III. We Must Be Thankful for Salvation.

God's grace is so great that we can scarcely understand it. But a simple story may help: Jordan was a shy third-grader, and artwork was his weakness. A crayon just wouldn't cooperate with him, and he could never stay within the lines. Even his friends laughed at his pictures.

One November afternoon, his teacher stood at the front of the class with a stack of white papers in hand. Jordan felt his heart in his throat. He knew an art assignment when he saw one.

"Class," she began, "I want each one to take a paper turkey. Put your name at the top of the page, color the turkey, and pass it to the front when I ask for them. We will hang them around the room until Visitors' Day."

Jordan felt his heart drop into his sneakers. With your names in plain sight, it would be impossible for you to deny your work.

Jordan's test papers had been hung. That was okay, but with this artwork up there, he would be known forever as "the boy who couldn't color turkeys."

He dared not appeal to his teacher. She was a thirty year veteran of crayon turkeys. Born to teach, her face was crowned by gray hair pulled into a bun. She wore rimless glasses and made red marks on papers.

Jordan knew he was doomed. He colored the hateful thing with his best brown crayon and hoped that somehow this time his picture would look like all the others.

Jordan handed his turkey forward to his best friend in the world. But even that friend looked at the picture and said, "Your turkey looks like an explosion in a feather factory."

Jordan watched as his turkey moved on. He wished it would disappear. Instead, it wound up on the top of the pile. This happened because each pupil along the way had to find it and giggle.

Finally, the teacher looked at the name on the ugly bird and shook her head.

Jordan left school with a heavy heart, knowing on Monday that turkey on the wall would condemn him to ridicule.

On Sunday, Jordan's regular Sunday school teacher was absent. None other than his schoolteacher took her place. "Boys and girls," she began, "the lesson today is about grace. Grace means God does things for us we cannot do for ourselves. This does not mean we do not try our best. But it means when we fail, God loves us enough to help us."

To Jordan, Sunday school stuff was not important when you knew a room of third-graders was going to laugh at you for a month.

All too soon, it was Monday morning and time for school. Jordan hoped his turkey had gotten lost or put in a corner so people couldn't see it.

But no such luck; the turkey was still there. No one could miss it!

Jordan approached his picture as a dog stalks a skunk. Then he noticed something. His turkey was not ugly. Someone had lightened the dark spots, filled in the missed spots, cut out the turkey, and glued it on a fresh white background. His turkey was new, brown, and beautiful.

He looked up at his teacher. Her mouth seemed to smile, and her head nodded slightly.

At that moment, before an altar with thirty turkeys, Jordan came to understand "grace."

That's what God does for us. Paul said, "All have sinned and fall short of the glory of God; they are now justified by his grace as a gift, through the redemption that is in Christ Jesus" (Rom 3:23–24).

"For if the many died through the one man's trespass, much more surely have the grace of God and the free gift in the grace of the one man, Jesus Christ, abounded for the many" (Rom 5:15b).

We must be thankful for salvation.

An Ungrateful Heart
Luke 17:11-19

Thanksgiving is a season for gratitude and appreciation. Luke tells us an amazing story about that. He says, "As [Jesus] entered a village, ten lepers approached him. Keeping their distance" (Luke 17:12).

These ten outcasts in this little town knew their place. It's significant that even with Jesus, they kept their distance. They didn't dare approach. Leprosy was contagious. People with this terrible disease felt dirty and unwanted. They were forbidden to associate with other people.

Nevertheless, they could still talk: "Jesus, Master, have mercy on us!" (Luke 17:13).

They were loud in their pleas for help. "When he saw them, he said to them, 'Go and show yourselves to the priests.' And as they went, they were made clean" (Luke 17:14).

Jesus never ignored an honest cry for help. He heard them and saw them, but his response was rather strange. Instead of touching them or teaching them, he followed tradition and said, "Present yourself to the priests." This was the process to get back into society. The priests would inspect former sufferers and declare them whole. Jesus is saying, "Act as if you are healed. Go to the priests to show that you are cleansed!" His acceptance and love worked its miracle. They felt clean and thus became clean. This is a sound psychological principle. Act "as if," and it will happen!

"Then one of them, when he saw that he was healed, turned back, praising God with a loud voice" (Luke 17:15).

Perhaps they stopped on the road in their excitement. "Now that we're free, what are we going to do?" One said, "I'm going to see my wife." Another said, "I can hardly wait to see my children." Another said, "I had a good business at Capernaum and must tend my affairs." Another said, "I have some sheep near Nazareth. I must see about them."

One by one, they followed their personal interests and went on with their lives—all except one. The despised Samaritan said, "I have a wife; I have children; I have a little farm. I want to get back as quickly as possible, but there is something else I must do first." As he turned back to express his gratitude, we must notice that he was not actually obeying Jesus. He didn't go to the priests as he was commanded. Instead, his love and appreciation overrode absolute obedience. "He prostrated himself at Jesus' feet and thanked him. And he was a Samaritan" (Luke 17:16).

One came back! And Jesus said, "And he was a Samaritan!" This is the moral: The hated, despised, unorthodox one was the best one.

"Then Jesus asked, "Were not ten made clean? But the other nine, where are they?'" (Luke 17:17).

Jesus noted both the response and the lack of response. He said, "Were there not ten of you?" "Yes, there were ten." "Weren't the other nine healed?" "Yes, they were healed too." "So where are they?" That's a good question. Where in the world are they?

"Was none of them found to return and give praise to God except this foreigner?" (Luke 17:18).

It's significant that as soon as they got what they wanted, they disappeared. Isn't that human nature? As soon as our pain gets easy, we forget! But before we condemn these men for their ingratitude—before we say, "Look at those terrible men. God did so much for them, and they forgot"—let's consider this: Do we say, "Thank you, Lord, because I've never been sick with leprosy, I've never been ostracized, and I am blessed with good health"?

You see, our ingratitude is worse than theirs. God has been even better to us, and we've failed to acknowledge it. We simply take life and its blessings for granted.

A modern parable is titled "The Day the Sun Didn't Rise." The morning started as usual, but at the appointed hour, when the sun was supposed to rise, it didn't show up. Seven, eight, nine o'clock came and still no sun. People wandered around in the darkness and cried. People gathered in the churches and prayed, "Oh, God, what a disaster has come upon us. The sun did not rise this morning."

God heard their prayers, and the next morning, at the appointed hour, the sun was in its place. The people all said, "Thank you, Lord, for giving us a bright new day." Until they had lost the sun, it never occurred to them to thank God for it.

Do we forget our daily blessings? Do we get out of bed saying, "Thank you, Lord, for a new day, for life, for family, for friends, and for a church"?

You see, ingratitude is born out of complacency. It has always happened! So it will just keep on happening! We don't become aware of the good until we experience the bad. We "don't miss the water until the well runs dry"!

Now, what keeps us from being sensitive, appreciative, and grateful?

I. Greed

We're like the lepers. Most of us do more asking than we do thanking. One postmaster counted the letters of children who wrote to ask Santa for things and then counted the letters of those who wrote to thank Santa for what they had received. There were thousands of letters asking for something, but there was only one card of thanks.

Greed destroys gratitude. Greed is deceiving. No matter how much we have, it's never enough. The scripture says, "You have sown much, and harvested little; you eat, but you never have enough; you drink, but you never have your fill; you clothe yourselves, but no one is warm; and you that earn wages earn wages to put them into a bag with holes" (Hag 1:6).

We are selfish and greedy.

II. Envy

A little boy was proud of his new bicycle until he discovered his best friend had gotten a ten speed. A teenager was very happy about getting a cellphone until she learned her friend had received a smartphone. A woman was very pleased to get a job until she found out her friend had gotten a higher paying job.

Envy destroys gratitude. We see what others have and say, "I wish I had that." These desires make us ungrateful for what we do have.

Solomon said, "The lover of money will not be satisfied with money; nor the lover of wealth, with gain" (Eccl 5:10).

Envy is useless.

III. Complacency

We take things for granted. Once, there was a couple who had six children. All of them needed new shoes, and at about the same time, their washing machine broke down. The father was working part time and very short on cash, so he placed an ad for a used machine. When he heard of one and went to get it, he noticed the home was lavishly furnished. The conversation got around to children, and he commented on the problems of feeding and clothing six children. He especially griped about having to buy six new pairs of shoes.

At that, the woman ran out of the room crying. Her husband explained that they only had one child, and he had been paralyzed and bedfast from birth, and therefore had never needed a pair of shoes. When the poor man got home, he picked up all the little shoes, scuffed from kicking rocks and jumping puddles. He held him in his hands and thanked God for the privilege of replacing worn-out shoes. It's so easy to take our blessings for granted. It's so easy to become complacent. As soon as our fear or need is gone, we forget! It seems that promises made in foxholes are forgotten on V-day.

Are we like the nine ungrateful lepers—greedy, envious, and complacent? Or are we like the one grateful Samaritan who came back? Are we appreciative? Are we grateful?

Let's not forget to give thanks for our blessings!

Thankful Thoughts

Philippians 4:8

If you were on vacation and heard your house had burned down and all of your possessions were lost but then you arrived at the scene and found out it wasn't your house after all, how would you feel?

If a hurricane swept through and destroyed almost everything in your area but somehow left your buildings untouched, how would you feel?

If you received word that the plane your son was supposed to be on had crashed but then heard his voice on the phone telling you he had missed the flight, how would you feel?

Well, those feelings you had were called thankfulness, gratitude, and appreciation. This is the season to understand and activate those feelings. Feelings are affected by thoughts.

The power of thought is tremendous. Recently, a school gave elementary pupils a new test of learning ability. After the tests were graded, the teachers were given the names of five children in each class who were designated as "gifted," possessing exceptional learning ability.

The teachers didn't know that these names had been picked on a completely random basis before the tests were given. Any difference between the chosen few and the others existed only in the minds of the teachers.

Even so, tests taken at the end of the school year revealed that these "gifted" pupils had indeed moved far ahead of the other children, gaining as many as twenty IQ points. Furthermore, the teachers described them as more affectionate and potentially more successful. Obviously, the only change was one of attitude. Because the teachers expected more of certain students, these students began to expect more of themselves. Your mind affects your life.

The most important things in life are invisible. There is nothing more real than love and hate and fear and courage. There is nothing more real than the thoughts of the mind and the meditations of the heart.

Yes, thoughts are real things. In fact, Jesus equated evil thoughts with actual crimes. He said, "For out of the heart come evil intentions, murder, adultery, fornication, theft, false witness, slander. These are what defile a person" (Matt 15:19–20).

We wouldn't dream of putting water in our gas tank, but we do something even worse every time we put an evil, idle, or negative thought into our minds.

We are responsible for our thoughts.

Furthermore, Paul said thoughts transform our lives: "Do not be conformed to this world, but be transformed by the renewing of your minds, so that you may discern what is the will of God—what is good and acceptable and perfect" (Rom 12:2).

So how can we choose our thoughts and thereby shape our lives?

I. Reject Evil Thoughts.

Paul said a loving person "is patient...kind...is not envious or boastful or arrogant or rude...does not insist on [one's] own way...is not irritable or resentful...does not rejoice in wrongdoing, but rejoices in the truth" (1 Cor 13:4-6).

Thoughts are mental magnets, and like attracts like. If we think evil, we'll inevitably bring evil into our lives. The only water that can sink a ship is the water that gets inside. It's the same with evil. The only evil that can destroy us is the evil that gets inside, and in most cases it enters through our thoughts.

What is an evil thought? Well, cynicism and hostility are evil. When the angry scribes said to themselves that he was a blasphemer, Jesus, knowing their thoughts, responded, "Why do you think evil in your hearts?" (Matt 9:4).

Greed and ulterior motives are evil. When Simon the sorcerer wanted to buy the Holy Spirit in order to use the power for profit, Peter said, "May your silver perish with you, because you thought you could obtain God's gift with money!" (Acts 8:20).

Prejudice and discrimination are evil. James said, "If you take notice of the one wearing the fine clothes and say, 'Have a seat here, please,' while to the one who is poor you say, 'Stand there,' or, 'Sit at my feet,' have you not made distinctions among yourselves, and become judges with evil thoughts?" (Jas 2:3–4).

We must learn to "change channels" immediately when we find ourselves entertaining evil thoughts, because the longer they remain, the more damage they will do and the harder they will be to remove.

II. Reject Negative Thoughts.

Paul not only advocated positive thinking; he specifically defined it when he said, "Finally, beloved, whatever is true, whatever is honorable, whatever is just, whatever is pure, whatever is pleasing, whatever is commendable, if there is any excellence and if there is anything worthy of praise, think about these things" (Phil 4:8).

Now, are we willing to evaluate all of our own thoughts by these criteria?

We gradually become what we think about. Very few people realize this, and consequently there is a great deal of carelessness in regard to thoughts. Some people who guard their words and control their actions with great care are remarkably unconcerned about their thoughts. It's as if we believe as long as a thing is not put into audible words or observable deeds, it is of no consequence. We imagine that since no one hears or knows about these thoughts, they'll do no harm. That's not true! Negative thoughts include guilt about the past and pessimism about the future.

Paul said, "This one thing I do: forgetting what lies behind and straining forward to what lies ahead" (Phil 3:13).

III. Reject Idle Thoughts.

The writer of Proverbs said even having trivial, idle thoughts is sinful. He said, "The devising of folly is sin" (Prov 24:9).

The term foolish means silly or irrational. Idle thoughts, like idle words, are a waste of time, at best, and a forerunner of unproductive behavior, at worst. What is an idle thought? Well, preoccupation with material things is idle. Jesus said, "Do not worry about your life, what you will eat or what you will drink, or about your body, what you will wear. Is not life more than food, and the body more than clothing?" (Matt 6:25).

Anxiety and insecurity are idle. Jesus said, "Do not worry about tomorrow, for tomorrow will bring worries of its own" (Matt 6:34).

Egotism and arrogance are idle. Paul said, "For the wisdom of this world is foolishness with God" (1 Cor 3:19).

How, then, can we control those persistent obsessions that run through our minds? Well, fighting such unwanted thoughts is useless. Jesus said, "Do not resist an evildoer" (Matt 5:39). He knew the more we try to attack a thing, the bigger and more insidious it becomes. If someone says, "Now, don't think of blue monkeys;" that's all we'll be able to do! Instead, we must use discipline. Substitute another thought. Get busy on a worthy project. Interact with a wise mature person. Remember, "Deep thoughts make a deep person."

Remember, God knows and analyzes our thoughts. Jesus said, "Nothing is covered up that will not be uncovered, and nothing secret that will not become known" (Luke 12:2).

The writer of Hebrews said, "Indeed, the word of God is...able to judge the thoughts and intentions of the heart" (Heb 4:12).

What we think about changes us, and then we change everything we touch. Our thoughts shape our character. That's why our inner thoughts and our outer deeds must be the same. Jesus said, "Either make the tree good, and its fruit good; or make the tree bad, and its fruit bad; for the tree is known by its fruit. ... For out of the abundance of the heart the mouth speaks" (Matt 12:33–34).

Let's express this as a simple allegory: There's a little room in each of us where the real self lives. A little weaver sits there in front of a loom and moves the shuttle back and forth all day. He is weaving the warp and woof of our character, and the material he is using is our thoughts. He can only use what we send him. So our attitudes and our outlooks determine our lives.

An important purpose of the Thanksgiving season is to remind us that gratitude is one of our best attitudes and being thankful is one of our best thoughts. That's what Solomon meant when he said, "As a man thinketh in his heart, so is he."

Once, a woman found a wallet at the post office. It was full of credit cards, personal photos, and money. The owner's address was nearby, so she headed to the place, thinking about how happy the owner would be to get the wallet back. The owner peeked out when she knocked, then reached out, snatched the wallet, and closed the door. The woman was stunned that there was no "Thank you!" As she walked away, she wondered: "Wasn't this unfair? Why should I give my best if what I do isn't appreciated?"

Does God feel that way about us?

Let's be appreciative and grateful for our blessings!

Let's have good thoughts!

Let's have positive thoughts!

Let's have productive thoughts!

Above all, let's have thankful thoughts!

Be Ye Thankful

Psalm 100

On the first Thanksgiving Day, the Pilgrims held a prayer meeting to thank God. They invited their Indian neighbors to share their turkey and pumpkin pie. Sharing always accompanies gratitude.

Thanksgiving Day commemorates a bountiful harvest reaped by the Plymouth Colony. It is an American tradition. It's older than the Declaration of Independence. It's older than the Constitution. Thanksgiving is the most universal and the most democratic of all holidays. Now, it's the twenty-first century, and Americans still give thanks for the same blessings that our pilgrim ancestors valued so highly in 1621.

We live in a land with more material things than almost any other. That gives Americans a special obligation.

Thanksgiving reminds us of how much we owe to those before us and those around us. Thanksgiving reminds of how much we have. It reminds us that ingratitude is a sin. Paul lists it along with other deadly vices: "For people will be lovers of themselves, lovers of money, boasters, arrogant, abusive, disobedient to their parents, ungrateful, unholy, inhuman, implacable, slanderers, profligates, brutes, haters of good, treacherous, reckless, swollen with conceit, lovers of pleasure rather than lovers of God" (2 Tim 3:2–4).

In fact, Paul says, "Let the peace of Christ rule in your hearts…. And be thankful" (Col 3:15).

If you are an average American, you are tremendously blessed! But are you really thankful? Most of us take our blessings for granted and assume that we will always have them!

If you own a Bible, you are abundantly blessed. About one-third of the world's population does not have access to one.

If you can go to bed each night knowing that God loves you, you're blessed beyond measure.

If you have anyone on the planet, just one friend, who cares about you and listens to you, count this a blessing.

If you can freely attend church without fear, then you are more blessed than most.

If you have food in your refrigerator, clothes on your back, a roof over your head, and a place to sleep, you are rich in this world.

If you have an earthly family that even halfway supports you, you are blessed.

If you have a church family that offers you a word of encouragement, you are blessed with fellowship.

Yes, we take our blessings for granted. Husbands take wives for granted—their neat houses, their clean beds, their wholesome meals are not appreciated.

Wives take husbands for granted—their faithfulness, their hard work, their responsible jobs are not appreciated.

Children take their kind and generous parents for granted until they are left alone with only two graves and memories.

This is wrong! Writers are unanimous in pointing to ingratitude as a sin. Shakespeare branded ingratitude as the worst of all vices. He said, "I hate ingratitude more in man than lying...drunkenness, or taint of vice."

Unless we appreciate the small, daily blessings, greater blessings cannot come. A gardener once decided that since there were two pints of raspberries to pick each day, much time and energy could be saved by picking the raspberries once a week, all fourteen pints at once. However, after waiting a week to pick, there were only two pints to harvest.

The gardener realized that because I didn't harvest my raspberries on a daily basis, he lost them. Some raspberries ripened and fell to the ground to rot. Birds ate some. Many couldn't develop because the one before it was still in its place.

Until we learn to notice and appreciate and use the abundance that surrounds us right now, we won't be receptive to additional abundance. So how do we learn to appreciate what we have?

Let's notice and appreciate some of our many blessings by analyzing the word T-H-A-N-K-F-U-L!

T stands for time.

They say that on her death bed, Queen Victoria whispered, "My kingdom for an hour." We're not thankful for time until it begins to run out.

To realize the value of one year, ask a student who has failed a grade. To realize the value of one month, ask a mother who has given birth to a premature baby. To realize the value of one hour, ask lovers who are waiting to meet. To realize the value of one minute, ask a person who missed a train.

To realize the value of one second, ask the person who won a silver medal at the Olympics.

Let's treasure every moment and be thankful for time.

H stands for health.

Again, we're not thankful for health until we begin to lose it. One woman sent out notes saying, "You are invited to a 'Praise the Lord Dinner,' February 9 at 7:00 p.m." She said, "My family and friends all knew why this celebration was being held. I had just been released from the hospital and given a clean bill of health after a very bad scare."

Let's not wait for an emergency to occur. Let's enjoy our life and be thankful for our health.

A stands for abilities.

All of us have numerous abilities that are taken for granted. A person who had a deaf friend said, "I can't help her, but at least I can quit complaining about loud music, slammed doors, and street racket. I can appreciate my ability to hear laughter, squawking geese, and babies crying." If we can hear and see and stand and walk, we are very fortunate, and we should be thankful for these simple abilities.

N stands for nature.

Courtlandt W. Sayres wrote:

> One midnight, deep in starlight still
> I dreamed that I received this bill:
> Five thousand breathless dawns, all new;
> Five thousand flowers, fresh in dew;
> Five thousand sunsets, wrapped in gold;
> One million snowflakes, served ice cold;
> One hundred music-haunted dreams,
> Of moon-drenched roads and flowing streams;
> Of prophesying winds and trees;
> Of silent stars and drowsing bees;
> I wondered when I waked at day,
> How, in God's name, I could ever pay!
> —"Bankrupt"

Well, we can't pay for the beauty around us, so let's at least be thankful for nature.

K stands for knowledge.

With books and magazines and newspapers and radios and televisions and the internet, the world is at our fingertips. Abraham Lincoln had to walk miles in the snow just to borrow a book. In an information age, we don't realize our blessings. Let's be thankful for knowledge.

F stands for family.

Are you aware that if we die tomorrow, the company or business we're working for can easily replace us in a matter of days, but the family we leave behind will feel the loss for the rest of their lives? And yet we often give more of ourselves to our work than to our family. This is an unwise investment. Let's be thankful for our family.

U Stands for understanding.

There is no gift more needed or desired than the understanding of friends. When someone listens to our words and shares our feelings, our joys are increased, and our sorrows are diminished. Friendships include trust and empathy. Let's be thankful for understanding.

L stands for life.

In one best-selling book, the author discusses the various crises that people face as they go through life. One middle-aged reader described feelings of remorse for wasting time on ultimately meaningless activities.

Let's not miss the most important things. Instead, let's be thankful for life.

An anonymous author wrote, "Few of us will receive life's big prizes—the Pulitzer, the Heisman Trophy, the Oscar. But we're all eligible for life's small pleasures—a pat on the back, a four-pound bass, a full moon, an empty parking space, a crackling fire, a great meal, a glorious sunset! Enjoy life's little delights. There are plenty for all of us."

Christmas

The Best Gift

Gifts can be one way of letting our light shine at Christmas. The gold, frankincense, and myrrh of the wise men were actually the first three Christmas gifts.

Unfortunately, today most of us are never sure of our choices. We're afraid we will give the wrong thing. We're afraid it will be the wrong size or the wrong color. Besides, too many "gadgets" already clutter our shelves and fill our attics.

Fortunately, however, each of us has gifts that the world desperately needs. And we don't have to shop for them or put bows on them. The best gifts are free!

I. We Can Give Attention.

Dale Carnegie said, "You can make more friends in two minutes by being interested in other people than you can in two years by trying to get other people interested in you." Just a little attention can light up lonely faces. But you must really care.

People don't need our religious advice. They need patience and understanding.

Listening well is not a natural ability. As with any skill, learning how to listen requires effort and determination.

Christian listening says, "Right now, I am here for you. Nothing else is important. I want to hear and understand what you have to say." Ultimately, listening helps a person understand himself better.

The best answers are those that people discover within themselves. That's why attention is one of the best gifts.

II. We Can Give Appreciation.

A man said, "I was grateful to my old teacher who went out of her way to introduce me to literature. But I had never expressed that gratitude to her." When he wrote her a letter of appreciation, he received a reply written in the scrawl of an aging woman: "I can't tell you how much your note meant to me. I am in my eighties, living alone in a small room. You will be interested to know that I taught school for fifty years, and yours is the first note of appreciation I have ever received. It came on a cold morning, and it filled me with cheer."

All of us have been influenced and blessed by others, yet we have failed to remember them with words of gratitude. William James said, "The deepest principle in human nature is the craving to be appreciated." That's why appreciation is one of the best gifts.

III. We Can Give Time.

This may be the hardest thing to give. In the main entrance of Johns-Hopkins Hospital there is a famous sundial that reads,

> The only hour within thy hands
> Is the hour on which this shadow stands.

To give time, we must be willing to be inconvenienced. Have you ever noticed how many of the significant personal encounters in Jesus's life occurred as he was "on the way" somewhere else? According to Solomon, "There is a time to be born, and a time to die." But it is the interval between these two times that is of infinite importance. God gives us time. We should use it for others. So what time is it? It's time to live better. It's time to forgive. It's time for kind words. It's time to do that kind deed you've been putting off.

All of us have twenty-four hours in each day, but we often waste them. That's why time is one of the best gifts.

IV. We Can Give Love.

A flower doesn't wait until somebody gets near or compliments it before giving off its perfume. Instead, it gives off its fragrance continually because that's its identity. We must love because love is our identity.

Christian love includes empathy. It rejoices with those who rejoice and weeps with those who weep.

Christian love includes daily concern. Pious words on Sunday can't erase cruel words on Monday, or deceitful words on Tuesday, or obscene words on Wednesday, or disrespectful words on Thursday, or critical words on Friday.

Christian love also includes action. People need to be hugged. People need a helping hand. People need an arm around their shoulder. People need a tender touch.

A poet Edwin Markham told about a godly cobbler who made shoes. One night, the cobbler dreamed that Jesus was coming to visit him the next day. The dream seemed so real that he got up very early the next morning to decorate his shop for the arrival of his great guest.

He waited all morning, but to his disappointment, no one arrived except for an old man who limped up to the door asking to come in for a few minutes of warmth. While the man was resting, the cobbler noticed that his shoes were worn through. The cobbler took a new pair from his shelves and made sure that the stranger was wearing them as he went on his way.

Throughout the afternoon the cobbler waited, but his only visitor was an elderly woman who came by struggling under a heavy load of firewood, and he invited her into his shop. When he discovered that she had nothing to eat, he gave her a nourishing meal before she left.

As night began to fall, the cobbler heard a lost child crying outside his door. He soothed the youngster's tears and carried her home.

When he returned to his shop, the cobbler was sad. He was convinced that while he had been gone, he had missed his Lord's visit. In his anguish, the cobbler cried out, asking why the Lord had not come. A soft voice told him: I was the man, the woman, the child.

Then the cobbler remembered that the Lord had said, "What you've done for the least of these, you've done for me." Love is the best gift!

Attention, appreciation, time, and love—these are the gifts people want. They cost nothing, and yet they cost everything.

So let's remember to keep our light shining during this season and honor the Christ child who was born on Christmas day.

What Is Christmas All About?
Acts 1:8; 1 John 4:17

Christmas celebrates the time when Jesus entered the earthly realm. But Christmas is more than that. It also has a message for us as individual Christians.

As a believer, you have the spirit of God living in you, and you carry him everywhere you go: "As He is, so are we in this world" (1 John 4:17b).

As a believer, you represent the presence of Christ. You are his presence at the grocery store, at the gas station, and at the airport when your flight is cancelled. You are the presence of Christ at the restaurant when the service stinks. You are the presence of Christ at home where they know the real you. You are the presence of Christ when that off-color joke is told in your circle of friends. You are the presence of Christ to your children and grandchildren. Because Christ lives in you, you are his presence no matter where you are.

Jesus knew getting his message to the world would be a great responsibility. That's why he said, "You will be my witnesses in Jerusalem, in all Judea and Samaria, and to the ends of the earth" (Acts 1:8).

What are witnesses? What does a witness in a court of law do? Well, it's obvious that a witness is not a member of the jury. A witness is not expected to determine guilt or innocence. A witness is not the judge. He's not expected to sentence the criminal. A witness is not an executioner. He's not expected to carry out the punishment.

Instead, the crucial role of a witness is simply to provide evidence. So when Jesus commanded us to be witnesses, he didn't mean for us to be jurors. He didn't want us to determine other people's guilt or innocence. He didn't mean for us to be judges. He didn't want us to impose sentences of condemnation. He didn't want us to be executioners. He obviously didn't want us to carry out a punishment. Instead, he merely meant for us to give evidence of God's love and forgiveness and grace.

How can we do that? How can we keep Christ's spirit alive throughout the year, and especially during this Christmas season?

I. Our Good Character Reveals Christ.

No one will believe anything a notorious liar says. No one will be convinced by anything a known thief has to say. The testimony of a drug dealer or an alcoholic is taken with a grain of salt. So in order to be a credible witness for

Christ, we must possess good character. We must be reliable and responsible. We must have a track record that demonstrates integrity and honesty.

John said, "Those who believe in the Son of God have the testimony in their hearts" (1 John 5:10a).

Edgar Guest said in his poem, "Sermons We See,"

> I'd rather see a sermon than to hear one any day.
> I'd rather one would walk with me than merely tell the way.

> And the lecture you deliver may be very wise and true,
> But I'd rather get my lessons by observing what you do;
> For I might misunderstand you and the high advise you give,
> But there's no misunderstanding how you act and how you live.

Our best witness is our example! Solomon said, "The fruit of the righteous is a tree of life, but violence takes lives away" (Prov 11:30).

Paul said, "So that you may be blameless and innocent, children of God without blemish in the midst of a crooked and perverse generation, in which you shine like stars in the world" (Phil 2:15).

Jesus said, "In the same way, let your light shine before others, so that they may see your good works and give glory to your Father in heaven" (Matt 5:16).

Our good character determines our worth as a witness!

II. Our Honest Speech Reveals Christ.

People will not listen to hearsay. They will not be persuaded by our testimony about what others think. They won't even be moved by things we quote from the scriptures. People will only listen to our personal story, told in our own words. Everyone has an individual salvation experience. This is our gospel! This is our good news to share! We must be sincere and truthful about our sins and our conversion. Nothing is as powerful or helpful as a first-person account of God's grace. Each individual meets the Lord and makes his decision for Christ in a unique way. Like snowflakes, no two salvation experiences are exactly alike. Paul's conversion was very different from Peter's. Nicodemus's encounter was very different from that of the thief on the cross. Each of us has our own special story to tell.

Daniel said, "Those who are wise shall shine like the brightness of the sky, and those who lead many to righteousness, like the stars forever and ever" (Dan 12:3).

Peter said, "Always be ready to make your defense to anyone who demands from you an accounting for the hope that is in you; yet do it with gentleness and reverence" (1 Pet 3:15–16)

Jesus said, "Everyone therefore who acknowledges me before others, I also will acknowledge before my Father in heaven" (Matt 10:32).

Our honest speech determines our worth as a witness!

III. Our Compassionate Actions Reveal Christ.

People will not be influenced by idle, lazy, or nonproductive Christians. We are constantly being evaluated by our works and our service to others. How you relate to your spouse is a Christian witness. How you care for your children is a Christian witness. How you perform your job is a Christian witness. How you treat your neighbors and associates is a Christian witness.

Once, an old man was very hostile to religion and the church. The pastor and other members invited him to services, but he seldom came. When he got sick, they visited and prayed with him. Deacons read the scriptures to him. Nothing seemed to have any effect.

As time passed, he became needy and bedfast. The church began to take him food and other necessities. Finally, the preacher had to be out of town for a period of time, but he arranged for a caterer to provide meals for the poor fellow every day. Unfortunately, the old man died before the minister returned, but he left a message. He said, "Tell that preacher that I've changed. I've finally made my peace with the Lord. But it wasn't the sermons that did it. It wasn't the Scripture verses that did it. It wasn't the prayers that did it. It was the pork chops."

Sometimes it's our thoughtful deeds and kind actions that are our most effective witness.

Jesus said, "The harvest is plentiful, but the workers are few. Ask the Lord of the harvest, therefore, to send out workers into his harvest field" (Luke 10:2).

So as we enter this Christmas season, remember that you as a Christian are carrying the spirit of Christ with you. You represent the presence of Christ wherever you are. You are expressing his truth through your good character. You are expressing his love through your honest speech. You are expressing his grace through your productive actions. "As He is, so are we in this world" (1 John 4:17b).

That's what Christmas is all about.

The Grinches Who Steal Christmas
Luke 12:13-20

Dr. Seuss wrote about an evil creature who decided to steal Christmas. This Grinch took away the gifts and decorations and food, but he couldn't destroy Christmas because it was in the hearts of the people of Whoville.

Today, there are still some Grinches that can steal Christmas:

I. The Grinch of Materialism

We spend and charge and compare what we give and what we get. Stores and catalogs and the internet are hyping so many gadgets that we don't appreciate anything.

Our priorities get turned upside down. We're like the chicken scratching in the barnyard, searching for food. She spied a lump on the ground and pecked at it until she uncovered a bright, shiny diamond. The hen cocked her head and studied the sparkling jewel. Finally, she kicked it away, saying, "If my master had found this thing, he would be happy, because he likes such baubles. But I would much rather have a grain of corn."

Now, that diamond was worth more than ten bushels of corn, but the hen didn't care. It meant nothing to her.

Sometimes we're like that. We value things that our Master cares nothing about and ignore things that are really valuable.

The Grinch can't get enough and wants more stuff.

But the Bible says, "Be on your guard against all kinds of greed; for one's life does not consist in the abundance of possessions" (Luke 12:15).

And "be content with what you have" (Heb 13:5).

Don't let the Grinch of materialism steal your Christmas. Learn to be content!

II. The Grinch of Hostility

Families fragment as conflicts arise and misunderstandings occur. There are arguments over where and when to celebrate. There are hard feelings over cards and gifts and money. We're never satisfied and wear a "chip on our shoulder."

One woman was always suspicious of others' motives. Even when a friend tried to encourage her by saying, "Your little boy was really good in Sunday school today," the woman replied, "Are you saying that he's bad most of the time?" When you say, "You sure look nice today," she says, "You mean I look awful most days?"

Because of her twisted attitude, this woman can turn a sincere compliment into an insult.

Viewing others through hostile eyes can sabotage relationships. Some people take everything wrong and turn everything into a conflict.

The Grinch assumes the worst in others.

But the Bible says: "Hatred stirs up strife, but love covers all offenses" (Prov 10:12).

"Whoever hates another believer is in the darkness, walks in the darkness" (1 John 2:11a).

Don't let the Grinch of hostility steal your Christmas. Learn to be loving!

III. The Grinch of Stress

It's unfortunate that the twenty-four days before Christmas make up the most tension-filled period of the year. There's so much to do, so many places to go, so many things to buy, so many meetings and responsibilities. Sometimes we lose our perspective.

Do you recall the nursery rhyme about a cat who went to London to visit the queen? Now, this cat had the chance of a lifetime. There are so many sights to see in London: Westminster Abbey, the British Museum, Buckingham Palace; the Marble Arch in Hyde Park. She could have heard the London Philharmonic or watched the changing of the guard. She didn't even notice the historic Thames River or enjoy St. Paul's Cathedral. Instead, she scampered around chasing mice.

This cat didn't even honor the queen as Her Majesty stood before her. Instead, when someone said, "Tell me about your trip," she replied, "It all started when I saw this little mouse under the queen's throne." London might just as well have been in any basement or alley. "I just chased mice."

Too often in our concern over trifles, we also miss the best.

The Grinch says to hurry and worry and rush.

But the Bible says, "And the peace of God, which surpasses all understanding, will guard your hearts and your minds in Christ Jesus" (Phil 4:7).

"Let the peace of Christ rule in your hearts" (Col 3:15a).

Don't let the Grinch of stress steal your Christmas. Learn to have peace!

IV. The Grinch of Depression

Psychologists see more people around the Christmas holidays than any other time. Suicides are higher. There's disappointment and regret and sad memories. Many people have a "blue Christmas." But God wants us to have joy.

One woman said,

> When I was growing up, we were poor, but we lived next door to a rich family. They had many things we didn't have, but they missed the joy Christ can bring—which we had in abundance. I remember one day my dad was playing his harmonica, and the rest of us were singing Christmas carols at the top of our lungs.
>
> Suddenly, my mom said, "We're making so much noise. We better close our window or we'll disturb the neighbors."
>
> Within minutes our phone rang. It was a child who lived next door. She asked, "Why'd you close your window?"
>
> "Well, we didn't want to disturb you," was Mom's answer.
>
> The girl blurted out, "You didn't disturb us. That's the most fun we've had in a long time! Please open your window."

The Grinch says that holidays are not joyful, but a reason for sadness.

But the Bible says, "Do not fear or be dismayed" (Deut 1:21b).

"May the righteous be glad and rejoice before God; may they be happy and joyful" (Ps 68:3).

Don't let the Grinch of depression steal your Christmas. Seek out the support you need to fully experience God's joy.

V. The Grinch of Secularism

A minister said, "I didn't realize how far we had strayed until one morning I asked the children at church, 'Whose birthday are we celebrating?' Several said, 'Santa Claus.' Then one child yelled, 'Oh, no it's not. It's Rudolph's.'"

We must get our priorities straight. We must put first things first.

The Grinch says to just be concerned with your own stuff.

But the Bible says, "Worship the Lord your God, and serve only him" (Luke 4:8).

"Set your minds on things that are above, not on things that are on earth" (Col 3:2).

Don't let the Grinch of secularism steal your Christmas. Remember the "reason for the season"! Honor Christ!

So during this wonderful time of the year, let's be content. Let's be loving. Let's be peaceful. Let's be happy, and let's remember that it's a time to honor Jesus. Don't let a Grinch steal your Christmas.

Why Is the World Dark?

Isaiah 9:2

"The earth is degenerating. Bribery and corruption abound. Children no longer mind their parents. It is evident that the end of the world is fast approaching."

This dire assessment of a dark world sounds like it could be yesterday's headline. But, surprisingly, this bleak prediction was found on an Assyrian tablet written almost 3,000 years before Jesus was born.

So, you see, it's always been a dark world. But the gospel has a remedy for that. The scriptures say, "The people who walked in darkness have seen a great light; those who lived in a land of deep darkness—on them light has shined" (Isa 9:2).

Our world does seem dark today. Let's examine seven areas that need light:

I. Politics Without Principles

Watergate prosecutors said, "In hours of listening to White House tapes, there was not a single reference to the seeking of spiritual guidance or prayer. Instead, there was the constant taking of God's name in vain."

We need to elect honorable men and women. We need statesmen who look toward the next century instead of politicians who look toward the next election. We need officials who consider the good of all the people, not just their own wealth and prestige. Our country can't remain strong if it has politics without principles.

Paul said, "Let us live honorably as in the day, not in reveling and drunkenness, not in debauchery and licentiousness, not in quarreling and jealousy" (Rom 13:13).

II. Recreation Without Responsibility

We are a pleasure-seeking people. We want to be amused and entertained. We want what we want when we want it! "Fun" is a multimillion-dollar industry. We spend much more on sports and theater than we do on education, science, and medicine. We will excuse obscene words and immoral behavior from comedians who make us laugh and athletes who win games.

Many people have too much idle time. Recreation without responsibility leaves us aimless and unproductive.

Paul said, "The widow who lives for pleasure is dead even while she lives" (1 Tim 5:6).

III. Learning Without Love

We have more information today than ever before. Facts are abundant, but compassion is scarce. Data is available, but integrity is lacking. Unless we use our education to benefit others, it's worthless and indeed may be detrimental. A wise man said, "It takes both knowledge and love combined to produce wisdom." Learning without love merely produces smarter criminals.

The scriptures say, "Knowledge puffs up, but love builds up" (1 Cor 8:1).

IV. Wealth Without Work

We've lost our emphasis on the work ethic. Patrick Henry shouted, "Give me liberty or give me death." The next generation shouted, "Give me liberty." The current generation just shouts, "Give me!"

We can't continue expecting wealth without work.

Paul practiced tough love about indolence and idleness. He said, "When we were with you, we gave you this command: Anyone unwilling to work should not eat'" (2 Thess 3:10).

V. Management Without Morality

Business is getting bigger and bigger. The income ratio of chief executives to average workers in major corporations went from 40 to 1 in 1970 to 195 to 1 in the 1990s, and it's over twice that today. The average CEO receives multimillion-dollar salaries while the laborers get minimum wages. Many businesses contaminate the environment, distribute pornographic material, and make products that promote violence. They do this even though the effects are disastrous because the bottom-line dollar rules.

When we have management without morality, the rich get richer and the poor get poorer. That's wrong! That's obscene!

Solomon said, "Do not rob the poor because they are poor, or crush the afflicted at the gate" (Prov 22:22).

IV. Science Without Spirituality

Years ago, General Omar Bradley said, "Ours is a nation of scientific giants and ethical midgets. We know more about killing than we do about living."

When ethical standards are absent, we create things we don't know how to control. We are like a child on a bulldozer—he knows how to start it, but not how to stop it.

Too many technicians only consider what can be done, not necessarily what should be done! Science without spirituality is dangerous.

Paul said, "To the corrupt and unbelieving nothing is pure. Their very minds and consciences are corrupted" (Titus 1:15).

VII. Religion Without Righteousness

It's hypocritical to claim that reading the Bible is a chore but reading a thirty-page newspaper is easy. It's hypocritical to consider an hour of worship too long but an hour of bowling or fishing too short. It's hypocritical to declare that we can't fit a church meeting into our busy schedule but we can attend concerts and sports events at a moment's notice.

Let's get real! We cannot honor our religion without righteousness. Paul said, "They profess to know God, but they deny him by their actions" (Titus 1:16).

Our church—and each of us as individual Christians—has a mission this Christmas season, and indeed every day of the year, to bring light to a dark world.

The problems we have can be solved. There's a wonderful promise in the psalms that tells us how. David says, "It is you who light my lamp; the LORD, my God, lights up my darkness" (Ps 18:28).

1. Let's put principles into politics;
2. Let's be responsible in our recreation;
3. Let's combine our learning with love;
4. Let's quit expecting wealth without work;
5. Let's emphasize morality in our management;
6. Let's add spirituality to our science;
7. And let's identify our religion with righteousness.

In short let's light candles in the darkness.

What If Christ Had Not Come?

Why do we present a familiar pageant every December? Why do we tell stories about shepherds? Why do we mention stars and wise men? Why have gold, frankincense, and myrrh become important offerings? Why do we describe donkeys, stables, and mangers? Why is it important to remember the birth of one particular baby that happened so long ago? In short, why do we celebrate Christmas at all?

Well, the world seems to need this season. Traditions of Christmas are carried out in almost every country of the world. The "peace on earth and goodwill" it brings are enjoyed by many diverse cultures.

It's a wonderful time of year. Gifts are exchanged, decorations enjoyed. Great food, joyful music, visits, and fellowship make each day special.

But what if Christ had not come?

There is a story about a minister who dreamed that in homes, there were no stockings by the chimneys, no wreaths on the doors, and no decorated trees.

On the streets there were no bells ringing. There were no manger scenes. There were no stained-glass windows. There were no church spires.

In the library, over half of the books had disappeared. In the museums, most of the art was missing. There were no hymns or praise choruses or Handel's Messiah. The Bible ended at Malachi. There was no gospel, no John 3:16, no promise of hope, no Lord's Prayer, no Beatitudes, and no love chapter.

At funerals there were no messages of resurrection.

In a panic, the minister woke up, and his despair was greatly relieved when he heard carolers singing "Joy to the World."

Let's not take this season for granted. Let's not turn this holy time into a frenzy of buying and selling. Instead, let us be glad and rejoice today because "Christ has come." He has brought all the assurances and blessings and teachings of his life and ministry. He has offered salvation to every person on earth. Let us remember the annunciation of the angel: "Do not be afraid; for see—I am bringing you good news of great joy for all the people: to you is born this day in the city of David a Savior, who is the Messiah, the Lord" (Luke 2:10–11).

Miscellaneous

Grandparents' Day
Deuteronomy 4:9

> Whatever you write on the heart of a child
> No water can wash away.
> The sand may be shifted when billows are wild
> The efforts of years may decay;
> Some stories may perish, some songs be forgot,
> Buildings in disrepair;
> But this graven
> record of time changes not;
> It lingers unchangeably there.

Someone said, "I've never seen an evil baby." A newborn is innocent—a blank slate. The family and society write on that blank slate and create positive or negative results.

Most of this shaping and molding is unconscious teaching. Grandparents are extremely important in the development of character and self-esteem in a child. Some studies suggest that children who have been reared near their grandparents and in good relationship with their grandparents have a greater sense of security and well-being than those who don't have that privilege.

In addition, grandparents typically seem to possess certain character qualities that parents have not yet developed. Many of these qualities, such as patience and wisdom, simply come with experience.

Children observe our lives, our moods, our dispositions, and our reactions. They absorb our values. So how can you as grandparents use your unique positions and roles to provide the best benefits for your grandchildren?

I. Be an Influence.

That influence can be either good or bad. Furthermore, that influence will be felt for generations. The scripture says, "The Lord, the Lord, a God merciful and gracious, slow to anger, and abounding in steadfast love and faithfulness, keeping steadfast love for the thousandth generation, forgiving iniquity and transgression and sin, yet by no means clearing the guilty, but visiting the iniquity of the parents upon the children and the children's children, to the third and the fourth generation." (Exod 34:6–7).

This doesn't mean God takes vengeance on children and grandchildren and great-grandchildren. Instead, it is simply pointing out the long-range consequences of bad behavior.

It's true that each person is autonomous and individually responsible, but it's also true that an apple doesn't fall very far from the tree. That means it's easy for attributes and habits to get passed on from parents to children. Genes are inherited, and actions are imitated.

For instance, children of smokers are much more likely to be smokers. Alcoholism seems to run in families. Boys who observe abusive fathers often become abusive fathers themselves. As grandparents you can set the stage for a strong productive family legacy, or you can be the one who stops a weak, unproductive family tendency.

Influence is important, and grandparents have a great deal to do with future generations. Russia was an atheistic, Communist country for many years. The leaders did their best to stamp out all religions, especially Christianity. But when freedom came, observers were astonished to find that the faith community was alive and vital. In researching to discover how it had survived, they came up with this explanation: "It was the grandparents. They held on and were able to influence their grandchildren."

One man speaks for all of us when he wrote the following poem:

I don't recall the lessons learned
in my young childhood days;
The sermons all escape me now—
Can't quote a single phrase.

I don't recall what books I read,
what prayers helped me survive;
I do recall my pawpaw made
my swing when I was five.

Researchers say there are about five major influences in a child's life: As a grandparent you will probably be one of those.

II. Be a Blessing.

The notion of parents and Grandparents blessing a child may seem strange to many families, but it's actually an ancient and respected custom dating back to biblical times.

Children need to be blessed! This is especially true for teenagers, who often feel misunderstood by their families. Many feel that nobody cares. The danger of this situation is that as these young people go looking for someone to fill the void in their lives, many end up being emotionally, sexually, and physically abused. Our society appears to have no shortage of selfish and evil individuals just waiting to take advantage of a blessing-starved young person.

An Old Testament story describes this: "When Israel saw Joseph's sons, he said, 'Who are these?' Joseph said to his father, 'They are my sons, whom God has given me here'" And he said, 'Bring them to me, please, that I may bless them.'" (Gen 48:8–9, 20).

This blessing means "to speak well of" or "to praise." It also includes love, affirmation, respect, and hope.

Children have many inadequacies and needs. They have deep, instinctive fears of abandonment, rejection, failure, and humiliation. As grandparents you can assure them of your presence and protection. You can encourage and support them. You can pass on the wisdom you have gained from experience. Scripture advises us to teach our children and tell them stories that include moral lessons. "Tell your children and grandchildren...what signs I have done among them—so that you may know that I am the LORD" (Exod 10:2).

"But take care and watch yourselves closely, so as neither to forget the things that your eyes have seen nor to let them slip from your mind all the days of your life; make them known to your children and your children's children" (Deut 4:9).

Once, a minister was speaking to a youth group, comparing life to a football game. He encouraged them to be successful and end up on the winning side. He was feeling pretty good about his presentation until one kid said, "But, sir, we don't even know where the goal posts are!" Grandparents, you can show them where the goal posts are by demonstrating your moral standards and being willing to practice tough love if necessary.

III. Be a Witness.

When Paul wrote to Timothy he said, "I am reminded of your sincere faith, a faith that lived first in your grandmother Lois and your mother Eunice and now, I am sure, lives in you" (2 Tim 1:5).

As grandparents your daily example of living the Christian life is your best opportunity to influence your grandchildren for their good and God's glory. Lois, Timothy's grandmother, displayed a sincere faith. She wasn't a hypocrite.

Grandparents can teach by example. They can also teach by sharing information. Grandparents can tell stories and bridge the generation gap. They can be a sounding board on issues and problems that boys and girls face. They can teach skills such as cooking or gardening.

Grandparents have a wealth of experience to draw on. As one senior citizen said to a teenager, "Honey, remember, I've been fourteen, but you've never been seventy-three."

When a famous man with many degrees and achievements was being interviewed, the emcee asked, "Now, what is your most important title?" Without hesitation he answered, "Grandpa!"

You may also give your grandchildren biblical explanations and practical applications of scriptural truths. The psalmist said, "But the steadfast love of the LORD is from everlasting to everlasting on those who fear him, and his righteousness to children's children" (Ps 103:17).

The Lord accused the Israelites of having sacrificed their children to idols (see Ezek 16:20). There are many references to this abominable practice recorded in the Old Testament. Almost without exception, whenever such a scripture is read in a Bible class, someone will exclaim that they don't see how anyone could do such a thing to their children. Unfortunately, for all our pious sentiments, there has never been a nation of people who have sacrificed more children to their idols than the people of America today.

What about parents who encourage their children to seek popularity through promiscuity; parents who, by their behavior, teach their children to drink, curse, lie, and break the law; parents who fail to love and discipline their children; parents who give their children everything they want but nothing they need; parents who are too wrapped up in their own lives to teach morality and take them to worship? How do they differ from the Israelite parents who sacrificed them to idols?

Too many of us sacrifice our children to the gods of our jobs, television, materialism, and social status. Grandparents, your children, grandchildren, and great-grandchildren need you as never before. Are you building bridges for them? Are you leaving your grandchildren a moral influence? Are you giving your grandchildren a spiritual blessing? Are you passing on to your grandchildren a strong and vital faith?

That's your greatest responsibility, and that's your greatest privilege. You must not fail in this task. The next generation depends on you!

I Can! I Ought! I Will!

Labor Day

In the development of mankind, there have been three great milestones. These same three milestones occur individually.

It is a great day for the universe when a human being realizes he has autonomy and says "I can!" This is the birth of liberty. This is the moment when we know we have choices and possibilities. Paul says, "I can do all things through him who strengthens me" (Phil 4:13).

Another milestone is reached when we realize responsibility and say "I ought!" At this point we become morally accountable and aware of right and wrong. Paul said, "'All things are lawful for me,' but not all things are beneficial. 'All things are lawful for me,' but I will not be dominated by anything" (1 Cor 6:12).

The last milestone, however, is the one that really effects change. It moves us from the head and the heart to the hands and feet to say "I will!" Commitment and achievement are then certain. Joshua made this crucial decision when he said, "Now if you are unwilling to serve the Lord, choose this day whom you will serve, whether the gods your ancestors served in the region beyond the River or the gods of the Amorites in whose land you are living; but as for me and my household, we will serve the LORD" (Josh 24:15).

I. Saying "I Can!" Promotes Confidence.

We realize we are not at the mercy of nature and fate. We realize we have choices and possibilities. We realize we can shape our own destiny.

God gave us this authority. The psalmist said, "You have given them dominion over the works of your hands; you have put all things under their feet" (Ps 8:6).

Walter D. Wintle expressed it this way in his poem, "The Man Who Thinks He Can":

> Life's battles don't always go
> To the stronger or faster man.
> But, soon or late, the man who wins
> Is the man who thinks he can!

As Christians we are capable. We have confidence in our abilities. We are able to say "I can!"

II. Saying "I Ought!" Promotes Discipline.

We realize our responsibility. We realize we are not animalistic creatures—required to operate by instinct. We realize that just because we can do something, that doesn't automatically mean we should do it. We have limits and obligations and duties. God expects us to make good choices (see Isa 7:15).

It's important to have standards and values. One therapist found that when he treated his patients as victims of external factors, their progress deteriorated. But when he began to hold them accountable for their own decisions and actions, they made a dramatic recovery.

As Christians we are responsible! We have discipline and dedication. We are willing to say "I ought!"

III. Saying "I Will!" Promotes Action.

We realize our own power to effect change. We realize we are not going to be given success. We realize that having confidence in our abilities and being sure of our ethical responsibilities doesn't actually accomplish anything. It's the "I will!" that tames the forces of nature and creates greatness.

The prodigal son made this important decision when he said, "I will get up and go to my father" (Luke 15:18). It's important to note that when this boy made a move toward his father, his father moved toward him.

A decision must be acted upon. Good intentions are worthless. The three laziest groups in the world are people who almost went to college, people who are going to write a book someday; and people who wanted to be very successful.

Just saying "I could do it!," "I should do it!," and "I aim to do it!" is not enough. We need action! Don't talk about it. Just do it! As Christians we must keep our promises and live up to our professions!

So which milestone have you reached in your spiritual journey? Have you realized "you can"? Are you ready to say "I am autonomous!"; "I am capable!"; "I am competent!"? Are you ready to say with Paul, "I can do all things through him who strengthens me" (Phil 4:13)?

Have you realized "you ought"? Are you ready to say, "I am responsible!"; "I am reliable!"; "I am obligated!"? Are you ready to say with Paul, "We who are strong ought to put up with the failings of the weak, and not to please ourselves" (Rom 15:1)?

Finally, and most importantly, have you made the decision to say "I will!"; "I am committed!"; "I am active!"; "I am persistent!"? Are you ready to say with Joshua, "As for me and my household, we will serve the LORD" (Josh 24:15)?

My Teacher, the Ant

Proverbs 6:6–9
Labor Day

No one is too smart to learn from others. Even small, insignificant things can teach us if we are willing to learn. Once, a very wise person advised men and women to take lessons from ants: "Go to the ant, you lazybones; consider its ways, and be wise. Without having any chief or officer or ruler, it prepares its food in summer, and gathers its sustenance in harvest. How long will you lie there, O lazybones? When will you rise from your sleep?" (Prov 6:6–9).

In observing these insects, there are at least three principles to note:

I. The Ant Works Without Supervision.

He is a self-motivator, a self-starter, and a self-evaluator. In short, he is self-disciplined. The scripture says, "Without having any chief or officer or ruler" (Prov 6:7).

Such characteristics are so rare and valuable. How many employees work just as hard when the boss is away? How many employees will voluntarily shorten their lunch hour or cut out their coffee breaks in order to complete an assignment? How many employees do more than is required without the incentive of bonuses or overtime?

Yes, working without supervision would dramatically improve the labor market in America. We could eliminate many managers, foremen, and inspectors. We could increase quality and productivity. We could reduce our national import/export imbalance. We could also avoid many tragedies. One worker went to sleep on the job and failed to secure the door in a ferry boat. More than 200 people died in the English Channel!

What a lesson in responsibility we could learn from the ant! Working without supervision is a sign of Christian maturity.

No great artist or inventor ever does his task for an audience or an overseer. He does his task for his own self-respect and satisfaction. Responsibility is doing the right thing without being told.

As Christians we need to be especially careful about responsibility. People are watching us; they want to see if we put into practice what we profess. Our witness at work on Monday can be even more important than our witness at church on Sunday. Paul said, "Whatever your task, put yourselves into it, as done for the Lord and not for your masters" (Col 3:23).

II. The Ant Accomplishes Worthwhile Goals.

He does not procrastinate. He has no empty procedures or aimless actions. He wastes no time. The scripture says, "It prepares its food in summer" (Prov 6:8). Such initiative and pragmatic implementation is extremely desirable. Mindless bureaucracy—with its red tape and endless, nonproductive busyness—is stalling all branches of our government. It is destroying large corporations. It is hurting people and wrecking financial institutions. Simple, practical efficiency would solve many of the major economic problems in our country. Someone said, "A committee is a small group of people who keep minutes and waste hours!" A Chinese proverb says, "If we don't change our course, we're in danger of ending up where we're headed!" If so, many of us are headed for the miscellaneous file or the trash heap because we don't define our goals.

Whether you have a goal or not, you are going to be somewhere by the end of today. You are going to be somewhere by the end of this week. You are going to be somewhere by the end of this year. You are going to be somewhere by the end of life. Whether you pay any attention to goal setting or not, you will be somewhere. The question is this: Are you going to determine your own direction and purposes, or are you going to let circumstances and other people decide what you are going to do and where you are going to be at the end of this day? At the end of this year? At the end of your life? Ultimately, the responsibility for where we get to is up to us. We must decide.

Once, a reporter met Buzz Aldrin. He said, "Mr. Aldrin, if you were alone in space and your engine broke down and you had one hour's worth of oxygen, what would you do during your last hour of life?" "Oh, that's easy," replied Mr. Aldrin. "I'd work on that engine!"

You see, accomplishing worthwhile goals is essential. No matter what the motivation courses tell you, just "thinking you can" won't achieve success. You must add knowledge, skill, determination, and energy to your positive thinking! When the pioneers reached a river, they crossed it. When the pioneers reached a mountain, they climbed it. When the pioneers reached an insurmountable obstacle, they overcame it!

What a lesson in initiative we could learn from the ant. Accomplishing worthwhile goals is the purpose of life.

III. The Ant Provides for the Future.

He puts into practice that crucial principle known as "deferred gratification." This requires vision, prudence, and common sense. The scripture says the ant "gathers its food at harvest" (Prov 6:8).

The difference between success and failure is often the person's willingness to wait for gratification. Saving for tomorrow—working now and buying later, instead of enjoying now and paying later—is an almost unheard of habit. Yet we're jeopardizing our children's future to have it before we've earned it. Credit cards, second mortgages, and national debts are the sins that will bring America down. Greed—not Communism or terrorism—is our greatest enemy. When people say "I want to make a million," they usually mean "I want to spend a million." These are two entirely different things.

Research shows that ninety percent of Americans who gain a windfall through the lottery or other unexpected source lose all of it within five years. Most of us are economically illiterate. An ignorant candidate said, "My fellow citizens, what we need to do in this country is to borrow enough money to get completely out of debt."

A noted psychologist was asked to give the reasons why so many people failed in their efforts to achieve success. The scientist gave the following frank and valid reasons: doing as little as possible and trying to get as much as possible for doing it; putting off until tomorrow what we should have done the day before yesterday; believing we are smart enough to reap a harvest of pay before sowing a crop of service.

What a lesson in prudence we could learn from the ant! Providing for the future determines our survival as a species. Yes, we need responsible discipline and foresight. Jesus said, "My Father is still working, and I also am working" (John 5:17).

If God worked and Christ worked, what on earth makes us think we can get along without working?

Jesus set down a wonderful formula for success. He said, "Ask, and it will be given you; search, and you will find; knock, and the door will be opened for you. For everyone who asks receives, and everyone who searches finds, and for everyone who knocks, the door will be opened" (Matt 7:7–8).

We might explain the verse this way: Ask (pray about it). Seek (obtain knowledge and guidance). Knock (get busy and act). Do something about it. Put feet to your prayers. Work!

When we ask and seek without knocking, we are just plain lazy! Pure laziness is so often the real problem. And laziness is about the last sin anyone will own up to!

In order for something to be accomplished, we must work. A theologian said, "It's a greater sin to not work on the first, second, third, fourth, fifth, and sixth days than it is to work on the seventh day."

"Go to the ant, you lazybones; consider its ways, and be wise. Without having any chief or officer or ruler, it prepares its food in summer, and gathers its sustenance in harvest. How long will you lie there, O lazybones? When will you rise from your sleep?" (Prov 6:6–9).

The State of the Church
John 10:7-11, 14-15

When the president gives his "State of the Union" address each year, he often has to hype achievements and skew statistics to make it look good. A successful church shouldn't have to do that. Church leaders should express appreciation for those who cook, clean, arrange the chairs, and fill the baptistry; for those who mow lawns and repair the doors and teach and write and visit and call and decorate; for those who manage the money, run the audio and video systems, and do a thousand other things that keep the ministry on track. Encouragement should be expressed for those who are faithful to fill the pews and listen and respond and interact.

Leaders must emphasize that the church is a body, and it needs every member in order to succeed. Some members may think they're not important, but they are! Paul said, "The body does not consist of one member but of many. If the foot would say, 'Because I am not a hand, I do not belong to the body,' that would not make it any less a part of the body. And if the ear would say, 'Because I am not an eye, I do not belong to the body,' that would not make it any less a part of the body. If the whole body were an eye, where would the hearing be? If the whole body were hearing, where would the sense of smell be? But as it is, God arranged the members in the body, each one of them, as he chose. Now you are the body of Christ and individually members of it" (1 Cor 12:14–18, 27).

We all have different gifts. Each gift came because of the grace God gave us: "For as in one body we have many members, and not all the members have the same function, We have gifts that differ according to the grace given to us" (Rom 12:4, 6a).

When members are missing or not functioning, it's like a person trying to get along without an eye or a leg. We must use our gifts, and those gifts are varied. Paul said, "We have gifts that differ according to the grace given to us: prophecy, in proportion to faith; ministry, in ministering; the teacher, in teaching; the exhorter, in exhortation; the giver, in generosity; the leader, in diligence; the compassionate, in cheerfulness" (Rom 12:6b–8).

Notice that he lists serving, encouraging, and being kind as equal gifts with preaching, teaching, and contributing money. So never overlook or discount your gifts. You are not only important; you are essential. The church must try to help people discover and use their gifts to further the kingdom of God.

It's unfortunate that many people define talent only as the ability to play the piano, sing solos, or paint pictures. Talent is any natural, God-given ability to do something well. For example, we can be cheerful and hospitable. We can have the self-discipline to finish projects we start. We can show our love by smiling and listening.

Everyone has at least one gift. Peter said, "Like good stewards of the manifold grace of God, serve one another with whatever gift each of you has received" (1 Pet 4:10).

The gifts are different, but each is important.

Today we have the ability to make a new start. Today we have a chance to begin a new life. Jesus said, "I came that they may have life, and have it abundantly" (John 10:10).

Jesus offers the kind of life that not only fills our eternal needs; it also fulfills our earthly needs. Furthermore, if our needs were truly filled, destructive addictions like alcoholism, drugs, and promiscuity would disappear. People who succumb to these vices are really trying to eliminate their emptiness, abolish their misery, and fill their legitimate needs.

Unfortunately, these things don't satisfy; they only create more problems. Paul gives us a wonderful promise: "And my God will fully satisfy every need of yours according to his riches in glory in Christ Jesus" (Phil 4:19).

So what are these deep, unfulfilled needs that make us miserable and cause us to destroy our lives? More importantly, how does the gospel fill these needs?

I. It's Natural for Human Beings to Judge and Rebuff Each Other.

Because of this, most of us have been so slighted and alienated over the years that we feel rejected. But Jesus offers total acceptance. He said, "Everything that the Father gives me will come to me, and anyone who comes to me I will never drive away" (John 6:37).

II. It's Natural for Human Beings to Criticize and Revile Each Other.

Because of this, most of us have been so hurt and despised over the years that we feel unloved. But Jesus offers unconditional love. He said, "No one has greater love than this, to lay down one's life for one's friends" (John 15:13).

III. It's Natural for Human Beings to Degrade and Dishonor Each Other.

Because of this, most of us have been so disrespected and humiliated over the years that we feel worthless. But Jesus emphasizes our value. He said, "Not one [sparrow] will fall to the ground apart from your Father. So do not be afraid; you are of more value than many sparrows" (Matt 10:29, 31).

IV. It's Natural for Human Beings to Intimidate and Threaten Each Other.

Because of this, most of us have been so intimidated and bullied over the years that we feel insecure. But Jesus offers absolute security. He said, "Peace I leave with you; my peace I give to you. I do not give to you as the world gives. Do not let your hearts be troubled, and do not let them be afraid" (John 14:27).

V. It's Natural for Human Beings to Blame and Accuse Each Other.

Because of this, most of us have been so shamed and condemned over the years that we feel guilty. But Jesus offers complete forgiveness. He said, "Anyone who hears my word and believes him who sent me has eternal life, and does not come under judgment, but has passed from death to life" (John 5:24).

VI. It's Natural for Human Beings to Be Apathetic and Undisciplined.

Because of this, most us have become so aimless and unfocused over the years that we feel frustrated. But Jesus gives us purpose. He said, "Go therefore and make disciples of all nations...teaching them to obey everything that I have commanded you" (Matt 28:19–20a).

VII. It's Natural for Human Beings to Experience Depression and Misery.

Because of this, most of us become so discouraged and pessimistic over the years that we feel despair. But Jesus gives us hope and joy. He said, "I have said these things to you so that my joy may be in you, and that your joy may be complete" (John 15:11).

It's obvious that every individual needs acceptance, love, value, security, forgiveness, purpose, and hope. If any of these basic needs are not met, we feel empty and incomplete. That's why Jesus offers salvation. Over and over during his ministry on earth, when the Lord met hurting people, he would declare, "You are made whole." He meant, "All your needs are fulfilled, and you lack nothing."

If every member discovers and uses their gifts, then the church will fulfill its mission. Each individual who attends services will be able to say:

1. "I was accepted by my church family."
2. "I felt loved by God and my fellow Christians."
3. "My work in the church gave me a feeling of value."
4. "I experienced peace and security instead of anxiety and insecurity."
5. "I was forgiven, and my guilt was abolished."
6. "My faith gave meaning and purpose to my life."
7. "I have hope instead of despair."

If something consistently produces such positive results, then it's real.

According to legend, the little boy who gave Jesus his "loaves and fishes" saw Jesus's miracle and said, "Wow! If he can do that with my lunch, what could he do with my whole life?"

Each of us could ask the same thing: What if I gave him my whole life? What if I gave him my time? Would my day look different? Would I get things done? Would he enable me to accomplish more of his work? What if I gave him my talents? Would I discover some hidden special abilities? Would he develop them more fully? Would he allow me to influence every life I encounter? What if I gave him my treasure? Would I be able to invest in things that will last throughout eternity? What if I didn't stop at time, talents, and treasure? What if I gave him my hopes and my dreams?

Jesus said, "Those who want to save their life will lose it, and those who lose their life for my sake, and for the sake of the gospel, will save it" (Mark 8:35b).

The church's motto should be: "Every member in service!" That's God's will for the state of the church!

The Christ Within
John 17:21
Palm Sunday

Where is Christ? Is he "back there" in the first century? Is he "up there" on some great white throne? Is he "out there" in some supernatural paradise?

Well, not if we take the scriptures seriously. Jesus said, "I am in my Father, and you in me, and I in you" (John 14:20).

Paul said, "It is no longer I who live, but it is Christ who lives in me" (Gal 2:20a).

Is Christ really within us? If so, how is he with us? Is he in our feelings? Is he in our thoughts? Is he in our words? Is he in our actions?

Well, if he is within us, then that means that we are filling the same role that he did. We are carrying out his ministry. John said, "As he is, so are we in this world" (1 John 4:17).

The Christ within is the part of us that is united with God. Jesus said, "The Father and I are one" (John 10:30).

When we consider this concept, we'll see the enormous and indeed surprising implications it has for our lives.

I. If Christ Is Within Us, God Expects Us to Be in Control.

Jesus said, "All authority in heaven and on earth has been given to me" (Matt 28:18).

More importantly, Jesus said, "The one who believes in me will also do the works that I do and, in fact, will do greater works than these, because I am going to the Father" (John 14:12).

He insisted that "All things can be done for the one who believes" (Mark 9:23).

Paul added his opinion, saying, "I can do all things through him who strengthens me" (Phil 4:13).

Being in control gives us a lot of freedom and a lot of responsibility. It means it's okay for us to think and decide and make choices. It's okay for us to try new things. It's okay for us to question the status quo. It's okay for us to analyze and adapt moral principles. It's even okay for us to make honest mistakes if we're willing to admit them and correct them.

Many Christians reject this belief about our autonomy and independence because they don't want to accept the responsibility it entails. They'd rather say, "This awful situation must be God's will" or "I don't have to show any initiative because God will provide."

That's not true! God doesn't accomplish his purposes without us. Even at the age of twelve, Jesus said, "I must be about my Father's business" (see Luke 2:49).

And now this is our business!

If Christ is truly living in us and working through us, then that means, with his help, we must try to correct evil situations. We must take the initiative and try to make things better. It means we are to be in control of carrying out needed changes in laws that affect people's lives!

II. If Christ Is Within Us, God Expects Us to Be Creators.

Jesus was a creator! John said, "All things came into being through him" (John 1:3).

Paul said, "For in him all things in heaven and on earth were created, things visible and invisible, whether thrones or dominions or rulers or powers—all things have been created through him and for him" (Col 1:16).

Now, if Christ is in us, then he is still creating through us! This means it's okay for inventors to make new inventions. It's okay for engineers to design new mechanical devises. It's okay for scientists to discover new theories, for musicians to compose new symphonies. It means artists may paint pictures, writers may write novels, theologians may interpret scriptures.

You see, God provided us with a universe full of possibilities. We have a planet with all the resources we need, and we are expected to use and develop those resources in productive ways. The scriptures say, "So God created humankind in his image...male and female he created them. God blessed them, and God said to them, 'Be fruitful and multiply, and fill the earth and subdue it; and have dominion over the fish of the sea and over the birds of the air and over every living thing that moves upon the earth'" (Gen 1:27–28).

We are not here on earth merely to exist. We are not here to meekly accept all conditions and circumstances. We're not here to be passive and apathetic. Solomon said, "Whatever your hand finds to do, do with your might" (Eccl 9:10a).

Paul said, "For we are God's servants, working together" (1 Cor 3:9a).

"For we are what he has made us, created in Christ Jesus for good works, which God prepared beforehand to be our way of life" (Eph 2:10).

If Christ is living in us, then that means we are responsible for carrying out his creative processes and developing productive innovations.

III. If Christ Is Within Us, God Expects Us to Be Ministers to Others.

Jesus explained his purposes, saying, "The Spirit of the Lord is upon me, because he has anointed me to bring good news to the poor. He has sent me to proclaim release to the captives and recovery of sight to the blind, to let the oppressed go free" (Luke 4:18).

Now, we're to continue his ministry of service to others. In order to reach and influence people, their guilt must be alleviated, and forgiveness must be offered. Jesus said, "The Son of Man has authority on earth to forgive sins" (Mark 2:10).

We may not realize it, but Jesus clearly passed this authority to forgive on to us, saying, "If you forgive the sins of any, they are forgiven them; if you retain the sins of any, they are retained" (John 20:23).

This means our responses and behavior affect the lives of others. If we offer forgiveness and love for people, then this enables them to recognize and accept the gift of God's mercy and grace. But if, instead of forgiving, we criticize and condemn people, these hurting individuals may never be able to experience the peace and assurance of redemption. Our attitudes, words, and actions are crucial in determining the fate of others.

Jesus spoke for God, saying, "My teaching is not mine but his who sent me" (John 7:16).

Therefore, if Christ is within us, then we too can speak for God. That's an awesome duty and also a great privilege!

If Christ is within us, this means we are to be in control of our lives and choices. It means we are here to create a better world. And it means we are responsible for reaching out to others with Jesus's message.

The fact that Christ lives in us is a permanent promise. Jesus said, "I am with you always, to the end of the age" (Matt 28:20).

Fortunately, Jesus gave us a concrete act we can perform to remind us of his presence. The Lord's Supper is a powerful symbolic portrayal of this important concept of the Christ within. Jesus explained it this way: "Unless you eat the flesh of the Son of Man and drink his blood, you have no life in you. Those who eat my flesh and drink my blood have eternal life, and I will raise them up on the last day; Those who eat my flesh and drink my blood abide in me, and I in them" (John 6:53–54, 56).

The Lord's Supper is a dramatic, concrete portrayal of our special connection with God. Jesus said, "I ask not only on behalf of these, but also on behalf of those who will believe in me through their word, that they may all be one. As you, Father, are in me and I am in you, may they also be in us, so that the world may believe that you have sent me" (John 17:20–21).

Each time we partake of the elements of the Lord's Supper, we are reminding ourselves that Christ is truly living in us. We are witnessing to the world that Christ is truly living in us.

The Meaning of the Lord's Supper

I. An Act of Remembrance

"The Lord Jesus on the night when he was betrayed took a loaf of bread, and when he had given thanks, he broke it and said, 'This is my body that is for you. Do this in remembrance of me.' In the same way he took the cup also, after supper, saying, 'This cup is the new covenant in my blood. Do this, as often as you drink it, in remembrance of me.'" (1 Cor 11:23b–25).

We are all aware of how an ordinary thing can become sacramental. Some simple pieces of red, white, and blue cloth, stitched together in a special way, represents our love of liberty. A wilted dandelion delivered in the grubby fist of a four-year-old and a dried rose from our high school prom become emotional symbols.

Jesus knew this, and he wanted to bring the meaning and purpose of his life into the ordinary moments of our lives. On the eve of his betrayal, Jesus and his disciples celebrated Passover in an upper room. He wanted it to be a special time they would always remember, so he blessed a loaf of bread and a cup of wine and shared them with his disciples. From the two most common elements of every Palestinian meal, he established his memorial. He didn't use costly elements because he wanted symbols within the reach of everyone. The bread might have been hard and dry, and the wine might have been bitter, but it would serve to refresh the body in the land of sparse wells. And both bread and wine would have been on the table of even the poorest of peasants.

So a supper became a sacrament.

II. An Act of Examination

Paul said, "Examine yourselves, and only then eat of the bread and drink of the cup" (1 Cor 11:28).

We must examine what's in our hearts and minds. Are we hostile, bitter, and resentful toward those who have hurt us? Are we envious and jealous of those who are richer or smarter or more popular? Are we anxious or greedy or obsessive? In order to truly worship, our thoughts must be centered on good, pure, and productive things.

III. An Act of Testimony

Paul said, "For as often as you eat this bread and drink the cup, you proclaim the Lord's death until he comes" (1 Cor 11:26).

Is our influence positive? Are we honest and open? Outwardly, Christians look like any other people you pass on the street. They don't wear uniforms and salute, like scouts or soldiers. They don't all have the same odd kind of hairstyle, like some cultists. They don't wear special rings or pins or have special handshakes, like the members of some club. They don't all go to the same church, or drive the same car, or listen to the same music. So you might say, "What's the big difference between a Christian and a non-Christian?"

Well, Christianity is not a bumper sticker or a "praise the Lord" sign. It's a seed of faith that is planted in the heart, Then it begins to grow and produce what Paul calls the "fruit of the Spirit." These nine characteristics—love, joy, peace, patience, kindness, goodness, faithfulness, gentleness, and self-control are the marks of a true Christian.

Do we exemplify these traits?

IV. An Act of Obedience

"While they were eating, he took a loaf of bread, and after blessing it he broke it, gave it to them, and said, 'Take; this is my body.' Then he took a cup, and after giving thanks he gave it to them, and all of them drank from it" (Mark 14:22–23).

Are we sincerely trying to follow Jesus? Does our life glorify God? Do we walk our talk? Too often, we're like the young man who wrote an enthusiastic love letter to his girlfriend:

> My darling,
> My love for you is so great that I would travel to the ends of the earth for you. I would fight my way through the greatest dangers. I would face storm and flood and fire in order to reach you.
>
> Yours forever,
> John
>
> P.S. I'll see you Saturday night if it doesn't rain.

Half-hearted obedience won't do!

V. An Act of Sharing

Paul said, "The cup of blessing that we bless, is it not a sharing in the blood of Christ? The bread that we break, is it not a sharing in the body of Christ? Because there is one bread, we who are many are one body, for we all partake of the one bread" (1 Cor 10:16–17).

Once, a father and son were looking at a picture of a twelve-year-old boy giving his younger friend a piggyback ride. Both boys were thin and ragged, but they were smiling.

Gazing at the photo, the son described the scene to his dad: "That's Juan and Mario. Juan was born blind, but he can walk; and Mario, who is on his back, can't walk, but he can see. So Juan gives Mario rides, and Mario gives Juan directions. They worked out quite a system. They're a team."

That's what Christian love can do when we share.

VI. An Act of Covenant

"While they were eating, Jesus took a loaf of bread, and after blessing it he broke it, gave it to the disciples, and said, 'Take, eat; this is my body.' Then he took a cup, and after giving thanks he gave it to them, saying, 'Drink from it, all of you; for this is my blood of the covenant, which is poured out for many for the forgiveness of sins'" (Matt 26:26–28).

Paul says a church family is like parts of one body—the eyes, ears, lungs, heart, arms, and legs must work together.

Along California's northern coastline there's a forest filled with some of the world's most majestic skyscrapers—the redwood trees. Strangely, these giants have unusually shallow root systems that reach out in all directions to capture the greatest amount of surface moisture. Seldom will you see a redwood standing alone, for high winds would quickly uproot it. Instead, they grow in clusters, their intertwining roots providing support for one another against the storms.

That's what the church is all about. The focus of the church must be on inclusion—reaching out to all God's children.

Now, if you want to remember what Jesus did for us, if you're willing to examine your life, if you want to give a testimony, if you want to obey Christ's command, if you want to share your faith, if you are willing to enter into a covenant with other Christians, let us celebrate the Lord's Supper.

www.ingramcontent.com/pod-product-compliance
Lightning Source LLC
Chambersburg PA
CBHW070843160426
43192CB00012B/2286